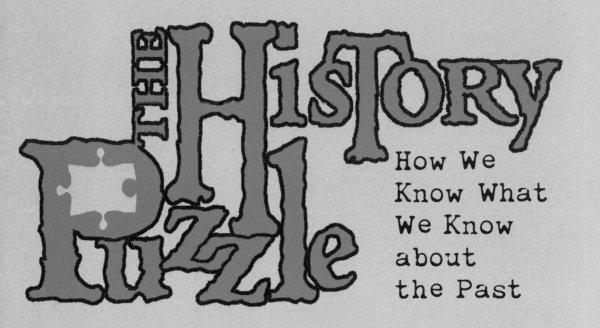

# THE HiSTORY PuZZle

How We Know What We Know about the Past

Susan Provost Beller

Twenty-First Century Books
Minneapolis

To my newest grandchildren, Katrina and Liam
—S.P.B.

Twenty-First Century Books
A division of Lerner Publishing Group
241 First Avenue North
Minneapolis, Minnesota 55401 U.S.A.

Website address: www.lernerbooks.com

Library of Congress Cataloging-in-Publication Data

Beller, Susan Provost, 1949–
    The history puzzle : how we know what we know about the past / by Susan Provost Beller.
        p.   cm.
    Includes bibliographical references and index.
    ISBN-13: 978–0–7613–2877–3 (lib. bdg. : alk. paper)
    ISBN-10: 0–7613–2877–7 (lib. bdg. : alk. paper)
    1.History—Methodology—Juvenile literature. I. Title.
    D16.B44 2006
    901—dc22                                                    2005017745

Manufactured in the United States of America
1 2 3 4 5 6 – JR – 11 10 09 08 07 06

# Contents

# A New Look at the Past

number of years ago, I visited Little Bighorn Battle-field in Montana with my daughter. I had read the classic story of Custer's valiant last stand years before, and the exhibits in the Visitors' Center illustrated the tale. The three-dimensional map of the battle showed the poor beleaguered general and his troops, innocent scouts, viciously attacked and overwhelmed by massive numbers of Sioux Indians. The command gathered together and died fighting on the hill in a battle known ever after as Custer's Last Stand. The battlefield markers emphasized the same story—signs along the way were placed to tell a certain tale. The only problem was that the story they told was at least partially wrong.

On a second visit to Little Bighorn some years later, I was surprised to find that the map and all of the exhibits had changed. Furthermore, visitors were now introduced to the site by a Native American park ranger who presented a very different story of the battle. What happened to change how visitors are introduced to the story of General George Armstrong Custer and his 1876 stand at the Little Bighorn? One event made all the difference—a devastating fire in 1983 that stripped off the hill's covering vegetation. That gave the National Park Service an opportunity to reexplore the battlefield. Using metal detectors, an army of volunteers mapped the location of spent bullets and other items left on the battlefield. A very different story from the one told in the history books emerged.

The mapping supported the written and oral accounts of the Sioux warriors who fought in the battle. These accounts had been ignored for more than a hundred years. The tale that I had learned as a child was one created by military leaders of Custer's day to gain support for their plan to remove all Native American peoples to reservation lands. The U.S. Army today still defends Custer and, in 1996, reaffirmed their belief that he acted in compliance with his orders and appropriately in the situation. Many historians, however, basing their judgment on the physical evidence of the search and the native accounts, present a different version of the story, one in which Custer divided his forces and attacked a much larger, better-armed force of Sioux and Cheyenne warriors—probably the largest gathering in battle of Native American warriors in Western history. As a result, Custer and his entire unit of 210 soldiers were killed. A shocked nation made him a hero.

The original version of the story, heavily argued by Custer's widow to protect his heroic image, ignored any evidence provided by the Sioux. Ignored, too, was the possibility that Custer disobeyed his military orders and sent his command against a force too large and too well equipped for them to withstand. Under the new interpretation, not only was Custer not the victim, it now appeared that he was the aggressor. When the natives fought back, he seemed unable to comprehend their strength and possibly guaranteed the massacre. He refused to withdraw while he had the chance, instead calling for another attack. He divided his troops, although he might have prevailed if the men had remained together. Taken together, the Custer of the Sioux accounts and the battlefield archaeology was a radically different Custer from the one I had learned of on my first visit to Little Bighorn.

Custer's Last Stand remains a controversial story, as fiercely debated now as it was immediately after the attack. There are still

The original account of Custer's Last Stand made Custer a hero, as seen in this painting from 1895. Many historians now believe that this was not an accurate account of the events of the battle.

those who claim that no native account of the battle can be trusted, and others who feel the Sioux accounts have a validity that needs to be accepted. One historian denounces the new archaeological evidence as tainted because "parts of the field had been corrupted by millions of souvenir-hunters" over the years, but he does acknowledge that it is time to study the native accounts that were previously "dismissed as the tales of cowards, liars, or incompetents." Other historians are busy studying the bones of the soldiers who died with Custer, attempting to verify accounts of the mutilations of the soldiers' bodies after death. One researcher notes that "the discrepancies between the physical evidence and the historical sources serve to reinforce the notion that not every witness is reliable or credible." This puzzling event of 1876 seems no closer to a satisfactory interpretation than it was even shortly after the battle. The new information may have changed how the history of the site and the battle will be presented to visitors, but historians have material here to argue about for many years to come.

How can this be? This event happened more than 125 years ago. Why hasn't someone determined the truth here and given us the "official" story of this battle?

Many of us think of history as fixed and unchanging. History books, in this view, need to be updated only to include the recent past. In reality, history is much more like science. It is a constant process of testing and evaluating evidence in light of the information we are gaining about the people of the past. Archaeologists are constantly finding new sources of information. The sites and artifacts (often called "material culture") that they find often lead to new interpretations of what may really have happened. The process of "making history" and how we go about it can be fascinating detective work as historians piece together the most detailed and accurate story they can to explain what actually happened. They may not always be right, but the process is self-correcting as new historians study the evidence and come up with new interpretations, or as new evidence is found.

We need to imagine that historians are piecing together a giant jigsaw puzzle. This puzzle is difficult because so many of its pieces are missing. Historians arrange the pieces that they have, trying to create as accurate a picture of the past as they can. Using this puzzle analogy, we see history as a process—something that all of us are part of. This history puzzle is one that we can help to solve. When we study the facts of an event, we are entitled to interpret those facts ourselves and create the most complete and accurate picture we can of the past. We, all of us, are historians!

## CHAPTER 1

# How Do We Know What We Know about the Past?

O ne of the greatest myths is that history is fixed and known. One gets the sense that everything of importance from the past is formally documented and unchanging. Most would admit that exact knowledge of the distant past is less certain, especially if we're talking about the time before humans began to keep written records. But many people have the sense that once written records were available, history can be easily determined.

In a general sense this is true. It is possible to determine certain "facts" about the past. For example, it is easy to set a date for certain events: William of Normandy attacked Britain in 1066; the Revolutionary War battle of Lexington and Concord took place on April 19, 1775; John F. Kennedy was assassinated on November 22, 1963; the Twin Towers of the World Trade Center were hit by airplanes and fell on September 11, 2001.

It is also generally easy to determine the who and where of history. Facts about these items are accurate from the time that records were kept. We may sometimes encounter difficulties in translating those earlier records into our own time frame. We may need to find some sort of key that allows us to interpret the record left behind. For example, the discovery and decoding of the Rosetta Stone allowed us to understand the written records of the Egyptians, to "read" the language with which they had documented their lives.

There is also generally sufficient historical information and evidence to allow us to rule out certain theories. For example, claims that the Holocaust did not happen are refuted by the overwhelming amount of evidence that proves that this event did occur. Likewise, those who try to prove that a moon landing was a hoax can be proved wrong by ample concrete evidence.

Once we move beyond the broad general facts, however, history becomes more difficult to pin down. What we call history is actually "made up." Good historians look at all the evidence available to them and use that evidence to make the most informed judgment possible as to what actually occurred.

The closer we are in time to the historical event, the more evidence historians have available to interpret the event. The further back we go into history, the less documentation we find and the more chance we have of interpreting events incorrectly. However, even the most recent events defy exact interpretation, sometimes through honest error, sometimes through misinformation, as happened in Little Bighorn. We need only look at what happened on September 11, 2001, to see how difficult this process of getting it right is. This was probably the most documented historical event ever, and yet, two years later, the final number of victims was still changing.

It is important to understand that there is no historical event about which we can be absolutely sure we have the right account of the who, what, when, where, why, and how. Extensive research done for court cases documents how even eyewitness

It's easy enough to determine that John F. Kennedy was assassinated on November 22, 1963, in Dallas, Texas. There are even photos of the event from right before he was shot (above). But it becomes much more difficult to determine the full account—the details—of this important piece of history.

testimony is not always accurate. Multiple eyewitnesses "see" an event differently. If this is true for witnesses to a car accident or robbery, one can only imagine how true it is for a major historical event like an assassination or a battle. Knowing that our eyewitness accounts today can be unreliable makes us realize that all of that first-hand information we rely on to interpret the past—what we call primary sources—is also somewhat suspect and needs careful evaluation.

So we have to approach history as less certain than it first appears to be. In addition, we need to recognize that history is being interpreted by historians. This means it is subject to each historian's point of view in looking at what documentation is available to him or her.

Historians face difficulties with the materials they work with. They may not know what bias is reflected in the primary sources they are using. When I wrote a book about the lives of women living in the Confederate capital of Richmond, Virginia, during the Civil War, diary after diary documented a very different picture of that war than I had found in Union sources. It was an eye-opening experience for me after having read so much material written from a Union point of view. The "perspective" of the primary sources was entirely different.

Historians need to evaluate each primary source to understand the perspective of the person writing it. On a recent television program about the Great Fire of Rome, in A.D. 64, one of the historians observed that the only eyewitness account of the fire came from the historian Tacitus, who had reason to dislike the Emperor Nero. That makes it important for historians writing about the fire to recognize that their primary source may be biased.

Historians themselves (and we too!) have perspectives from which they view events. No matter how carefully they try to be objective and reflect the whole story, their own interpretation and perspective creep in—in some cases, accidentally; in others, as perhaps at Little Bighorn, deliberately. Because of this, all of our history reflects the different perspectives of the people who recorded it. Moreover, the people who wrote the classic books about the past filtered out the overwhelming majority of information available to them. In an effort to be as "objective" as possible, history (at least until recently) prided itself on being based mostly on "official" documents. Such history was written from the perspective of government and leaders—it is often called the "Great Man" theory of history. Recently this has changed. Attempts are being made to reinterpret history through the eyes of people whose stories have long been neglected, such as women, minorities, and, in general, the common people.

What is history exactly? It is a compilation of all of the stories of all of the people who ever lived. The problem, of course, is that the overwhelming majority of all of these people never left us their stories. This means that historians are trying to piece together history from only a minute portion of the "facts" they would need to correctly interpret this information. The bottom line: It is very difficult to fully know what actually happened, even in the recent past.

## CHAPTER 2

# The Pieces of the Puzzle

**W**hat are the pieces of the past used to put together the best possible picture of what actually happened? There are three major kinds of sources. The first are written records that document the past, often referred to as primary source materials; the second are artifacts, physical items from the past that have been left behind. The third are historic places themselves, the locations where the events occurred. These three categories of sources offer different aspects of the story to the person who wants to interpret the past.

The best source of information for historians is documentary evidence. These are the eyewitness accounts of the past, written either at the time of an event, or during the later lifetime of people who lived when the event took place, or kept orally by a group of people over the years. Within these sources, those written at the time of the event itself give us the best source of information because they are fresh recollections and least likely to be altered. Take, for instance, two diaries written by women during the Civil War from 1861 to 1865. Mary Boykin Chestnut was a famous diarist of the Confederacy. She kept a detailed diary; however, before she published it some years after the war, she revised it, taking out and rewriting sections. Judith McGuire was another diarist living in the Confederate capital at Richmond, Virginia, during the war. Her diary was published in 1865, right after the war ended. Although both these diaries are useful to historians, the one published immediately after the war ended is more useful. Why? Because it reflects the actual views of an eyewitness to the events, without any later editing. It is raw historical material. It may certainly have mistakes in it—mistakes that might have been corrected if the author had waited several years to publish her work. But it offers a chance to see how this person thought about events right at the time, without her having time to go back and perhaps rewrite from later experience.

Among the documentary sources written at the time that are most used by historians, letters, diaries, and journals are the best, because they freeze moments in time for their readers. Other important sources are newspaper accounts and government and other legal documents such as reports, vital records, and land and probate documents. Historic maps and lists of various types, whether censuses, tax lists, or city directories, give us additional information. Yet another source of historical material, one that is also great fun to use, is known as broadsides—advertising from the days before radio and television. These one-page printed papers, which may have gotten their name because they were often pasted onto the "broad side" of a barn, cover such diverse topics as social events, school activities, electioneering, agricultural fairs, and traveling circuses and shows.

Among the most effective of "documents" are photographs

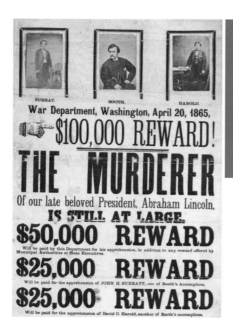

This is a broadside from 1865 advertising a reward for the capture of those who assassinated President Abraham Lincoln. Images of John H. Surratt, John Wilkes Booth, and David E. Herold are shown at the top.

This broadside from 1911 advertises a parade for women's rights in New York City. Historians obtain accurate details of historic events from posters like these.

taken at the time. Before the age of photography, historians had to depend on illustrations, drawings, or paintings of historical events. Such images often glorified historic events and protected people from realities, such as the horrors of wars. The first battlefield photographs ever taken were during the Civil War, days after the battle of Antietam, in September 1862. When they were displayed, viewers were shocked. These graphic photos of dead soldiers piled up in the Sunken Road, now called Bloody Lane, were entirely different from the newspaper illustrations that showed armies charging with flags flying and bayonets and swords flashing. The photographs had captured a reality that previously only soldiers had seen, and they brought it home. Similarly, in the 1960s television brought vivid pictures of the fighting in Vietnam into American living rooms.

Primary sources are wonderful tools for historians. However, as we move further back in time, their availability becomes an issue. Only recently has literacy become widespread in the population. In many early cultures, history and documentary information was not written down. Specially trained persons memorized the information that was needed to make the society work—the laws, the genealogies, anything required by the leaders to make decisions. From those oral accounts that survive, we know that these "records" were often fully as accurate (and probably sometimes more accurate) than early written accounts. However, they have one serious drawback. Although some groups maintained a strong oral history tradition, most of these

Photos like this one from the battle of Antietam, showing dead soldiers shortly before their mass burial, brought to the public the gruesome reality of war.

have been lost to us. As we move back in time, we find an increasingly small proportion of people providing the information available to evaluate the past. Such people also tend to represent only one viewpoint—that of the more affluent and educated classes of society. Moving still further back, we reach a time when there were no written records at all.

What can historians use to complement the written record or to interpret the past before writing came into being? They turn to artifacts, the material items left from the past. Some of these are a form of communication in themselves. Others are simply objects or, often, only pieces of objects. From these a story can be learned.

When the objects are recent enough, they are often used more to complement the written record. Historians tend to place more emphasis on the written word than on the physical evidence left behind, unless there is no written word. We have seen from our look at the bullet patterns at the Little Bighorn battlefield that artifacts have power in themselves to force a new inter-

The cave paintings of southwestern France, such as this one of a woolly rhinoceros, are a pictorial language that historians seek to "read" just as they might any other unknown language.

pretation of the written record. However, the primary way in which artifacts are generally used does not usually force such a reinterpretation. Instead, artifacts allow us to understand the material we are reading about. It is one thing to read, for example, an account of a surgeon amputating an arm during the Civil War. It is another to hold in one's hand an amputating saw that was actually used at the time and to know that that operation was performed with this saw. Historians use the artifacts of the past in order to make the past real for their readers.

Historians know that artifacts can also serve to solve the mysteries of the past even when there is a great deal of written evidence available. Thus the search for such recent artifacts as the luxury liner *Titanic* and the Confederate submarine the *H. L. Hunley* to obtain information from the objects themselves. There are times when the written record, no matter how complete, cannot compare with the physical evidence. The artifacts lend another dimension to the research. The combination of artifact and documentary source can not only aid in interpretation, but also reinforce the knowledge of the past by confirming its truth.

People need this physical knowledge of the past. We see people who involve themselves in "living" history activities. In some cases this is merely recreational, a chance to spend a weekend portraying a soldier living in camp or fighting in a battle, or jousting like a medieval knight. But often serious historians engage in such activities, or in even more complicated ones such as attempting to raise a modern Stonehenge or build a pyramid using techniques from the past. Art historians reconstruct the cave paintings of Lascaux, duplicating the materials and techniques used by the cave painters fifteen thousand to thirty thousand years ago.

Such activities seem to flow from two different needs. One is the need to do it oneself in some limited form to truly understand the reality of what one is researching. The other need seems to come from a realization that we often think of earlier generations as more primitive because their tools lacked the sophistication of modern implements. Doing things the earlier way gives us a chance to see that their thought processes reveal them to be our equals (and sometimes, it seems, our superiors) mentally, in spite of their lesser technology.

As we move further back into history, the availability of artifacts, as with the availability of primary source materials, becomes a greater problem. Right at the point when the written record is disappearing, the material record also becomes scarcer. Historians are more dependent on the artifacts that they *can* find. But the process of interpretation becomes more prone to error as written and material items from the past become scarce. With fewer pieces of the jigsaw puzzle available, we are less likely to come as close as we would like to an accurate finished picture or interpretation of the past. That is why historians, archaeologists, and others are always searching for more information and more artifacts. They want their interpretation of events to be as close a reflection as possible of what really did happen.

A historic site is any physical place where people have been in the past. Sometimes the site is easy to identify because records state that a battle took place and the building that is obviously old is still standing. At other times, we may have ruins to indicate where to search. However, in some cases, luck gives us the only clue that this place may hold historical information. Someone stumbles on a cave that contains paintings or bones or stone tools; the historian can tell that someone occupied this place at some time in the distant past.

Historic sites are often difficult to interpret. More recent ones will yield a great deal of artifact evidence and may even have a great deal of documentary source material to aid in the historian's understanding. For example, there is a house in Ferrisburgh, Vermont, called Rokeby that was continuously occupied by the Robinson family from 1793 to modern times. In addition to the house itself and its artifacts, there is a collection of more than fifteen thousand family letters that can be used to document the history of this site. The letters and the wealth of artifacts at

Ancient historic sites such as Stonehenge, built between 3000 B.C. and 1000 B.C., present historians with very few pieces of the puzzle due to a lack of written or oral interpretive material.

Rokeby make the task of interpreting the site much easier.

The historian viewing an ancient Roman site may be able to find at least some documentation to help in interpretation. However, as we move back in time to sites before recorded history, such as Newgrange, in Ireland, or Stonehenge, in Great Britain, the historian finds that the site itself must tell the story. The further back one goes the more the site and its artifacts are the only research materials available. We will see that this is why interpretations of these historic sites can be so hotly debated.

## CHAPTER 3

# Even Today There Can Be Mysteries—The Wreck of the *Edmund Fitzgerald:* 1975

In November 1975, a huge ore carrier—729 feet (219 meters) long, as long as a seventy-two-story building is tall—disappeared in a storm on Lake Superior. Superior is the largest of the Great Lakes. At over 350 miles (560 kilometers) long and 160 miles (256 km) wide, it is also the largest body of freshwater in the world. It is so large that it creates its own weather patterns. The Great Lakes are a natural shipping corridor for the industrial Midwest, and the *Edmund Fitzgerald* was one of the largest ore carriers working on the lake. The carriers have a relatively short shipping season because of weather conditions, and their captains live in dread of the infamous "gales of November," with their high winds and even higher waves.

In November 1975, the *Edmund Fitzgerald* was a seasoned boat with an experienced captain. She had made 748 voyages

The *Edmund Fitzgerald* on the Detroit River in 1974 before she sank

and traveled more than a million miles. When she left Duluth, Minnesota, and began her journey, the weather was beautiful. On this voyage, she was carrying a load of over 26,000 tons of taconite—iron ore pellets. A storm was predicted, but no one predicted that this would be one of the worst storms ever seen on Lake Superior. In the middle of the storm, only miles from a possible safe haven in Whitefish Bay and without time to put out a distress call, the *Edmund Fitzgerald* sank. All twenty-nine crew members were lost.

Today, more than thirty years after the sinking, there is still disagreement about why and how she sank. Several underwater archaeological dives have taken place to try to determine what happened. The question is still unresolved. The Coast Guard report on the sinking noted a number of possible causes, but concluded that "in the absence of any survivors or witnesses, the proximate cause of the loss . . . cannot be determined." The Marine Board of Investigation blamed the accident on "ineffective hatch closures," which resulted in flooding of the ship so

A member of the Coast Guard Board of Inquiry, Rear Admiral Winford Barrow (left), inspects debris from the *Edmund Fitzgerald*.

severe that she could no longer stay afloat. The official reports convinced very few that the definitive answer to this puzzling question had been found.

Today several theories for the sinking are hotly debated, with proponents of each accusing the others of trying to hide the truth. A large group believes that the hatches were indeed the problem. One writer notes that "securing the hatches required that, once the fourteen-thousand-pound cover had been positioned . . . the cover then be secured by sixty-eight manually positioned Kestner clamps. . . . A three-foot-long, two-pronged clamp wrench was employed to snap each clamp into place; the clamping process took two men approximately thirty minutes." Witnesses to the loading of the ship said that the captain did not take the time required to do this. In good weather, this would not have been a problem. But he then sailed into the worst possible storm.

Another popular theory is that "the *Fitzgerald* struck the Six-Fathom Shoal that lurks at and extends some distance north and east from the north end of Caribou Island off the eastern shoreline of Lake Superior." Some divers investigating the wreck report damage that could come from such an impact. But others say that Captain Ernest McSorley had more than enough experience on the lake to avoid a hazard like that. They note that the gashes in the ship could have come as she broke up and hit the bottom.

More unusual is the theory that the *Edmund Fitzgerald* was sunk by a Lake Superior phenomenon called "the three sisters": "That theory suggests that [when] the *Fitzgerald* was running with the northwest seas, three unusually large waves swept aboard from astern and met on her forward half. The combined weight of the waves then forced the *Fitzgerald* to bow under and literally submarine." The author citing this theory dismisses it, concluding that his own study shows no evidence of such an event.

Captain Dudley Paquette, who was traveling the lake during the same storm, claims that the sinking of the *Edmund Fitzgerald* harked back to an administrative decision several years before the event, when ships were permitted to carry heavier loads than they had originally been designed to hold. In addition, he claims that captains were pressured to carry the largest possible loads and make the trip in the shortest possible time, no matter what the weather. The result, according to Paquette: "A captain that loads right to those load lines and pushes his ship hard in every possible way . . . a captain that ignores very clear weather advisories . . . a ship that is loaded every trip for years with thousands of tons more cargo than her design called for? . . . Negligence!" Obviously, Captain Paquette brings his experience and strong feelings about this event to his account of it. No legal case has ever actually been made against the organizations that set the shipping rules for the lake.

Will we ever have a definitive answer as to what happened to the *Edmund Fitzgerald*? Probably not. A number of dives have been made to the wreck site. All the evidence that can be obtained with today's technology has been collected. There has been a series of official reports that do not completely agree with one another. We are left with a mystery with no agreed-upon solution. There is a great deal of primary source material here—testimony from captains sailing on the lake that night, testimony from engineers who understand the strains that a ship can and cannot withstand, and videos, photographs, and eyewitness accounts of those who have seen the wreck at the bottom of Lake Superior. With all this evidence, we can speculate on any number of issues. Did Captain McSorely misjudge the distance from the shoals in the storm? Should he have taken the time to make sure all the hatch clamps were fully secure once he realized they would be going into such a severe storm? Should he have taken a longer route and avoided the worst of the storm? Would the ship have fared better if not loaded beyond the capacity for which it was designed? We can also question whether a ship that had traveled more than a million miles might have suffered from unseen damage that would not show up unless she was faced with one of the worst November gales on record.

All the speculation will remain just that. Here is a mystery with plenty of documentation. All that is missing are the actual eyewitnesses. Those who were there went down with the ship. If we cannot solve this mystery with all the information we have, how much harder it must be to make sense of a more distant past.

## CHAPTER 4

# History Underwater— The Sister Gunboats of Lake Champlain: 1776

Only recently has real scientific archaeology underwater become possible. The finds being made and the information gained as a result are amazing. In recent years, underwater archaeologists have given new answers to modern mysteries such as the sinking of the *Titanic* and the loss of the ironclad *Monitor* in the Civil War.

Divers and submersibles have also provided glimpses of long-lost civilizations. A 1999 dive found two Phoenician cargo ships and evidence about the activities of the great Phoenician trading empire around 800 B.C. This fills "a blank spot in the archaeological record that stretches roughly from 1200 B.C. to 600 B.C." notes one archaeologist. Advances in science allowed for the recovery of the *H. L. Hunley*, which sank off the coast of Charleston, South Carolina, in 1864, "the first submarine in history to sink an enemy warship." Even recent losses of ships, such as that of the Russian submarine *Kursk* in August 2000, are followed by attempts to raise the vessel to the surface for further study (successful in the case of the *Kursk*).

A tale of two ships dating from the American Revolution lost in Lake Champlain highlights the amazing advances in underwater archaeological capabilities in the last seventy years. The story of the two vessels, the *Philadelphia* and the *Spitfire*, begins in 1776. The American Revolution was then at a critical phase. George Washington was trying to hold off a determined and much superior British army reinforced with German mercenary troops. The British developed a surefire strategy to divide the rebelling colonies and end the conflict. One army was to move south through the waterways of Lake Champlain from Montreal and meet up with another moving north from New York City, a British stronghold. When the armies met, the rebellious Massachusetts Colony was to be isolated, leaving the British the easy task of subduing the remaining, less rebellious colonies before taking care of those in New England.

The British strategy was an excellent one and only a limited number of ill-trained soldiers stood in the way of its success. American patriots built a fort at the narrowest point of Lake Champlain on Rattlesnake Hill across from the old French fort then called Carillon, now known as Fort Ticonderoga. With the new fort, called Mount Independence, and the existing artillery pieces at the old French fort re-aimed to meet an enemy arriving from the north, the Americans hoped to stop the British fleet. Since the British were stronger than the Americans, the Americans devised a strategy to slow the advance of the fleet. An American patriot with sailing experience, General Benedict Arnold, surprised the British by meeting them in the open waters of the lake with an American fleet. A hastily built fleet of gondolas and row galleys, under command of Arnold, was met by the British in a one-sided battle on October 11, 1776, near Valcour Island.

The Americans were, as was expected, defeated by the larger, better-armed British ships. But the battle bought the Americans some time. When the delayed British commander finally approached the two forts and found them fortified against him, he decided not to fight to conquer the forts this late in the season. Instead he chose to return to Montreal for the winter. His retreat gave the Americans a reprieve from attack until the following spring. Most historians believe that this delay may have made the difference between ultimate victory and defeat in the War for Independence.

In the course of the battle, several of Arnold's small fleet were sunk. Two in particular, the *Philadelphia* and the *Spitfire*, would be found in the twentieth century. Lorenzo Hagglund dragged the waters off Valcour Island with heavy chains in 1935, looking for the *Philadelphia*. It was located "lying upright in 60 feet of water" halfway between the island and the New York side of Lake Champlain. At the time nautical archaeological practice was to locate a wreck in shallow water and remove it as quickly as possible. Divers were limited to heavy suits without air packs (their air was hand pumped to them through a tube from the surface). The diving suits allowed very little visibility and almost no freedom of movement for the divers. It was not possible to carefully survey the area, study the wreck in context, and map the artifacts found.

The *Philadelphia* was brought to the surface in a sling on August 2, 1935. In 1961 the ship was acquired by the Smithsonian Institution and sent to Washington, D.C., by barge, where she can be seen today in the Museum of American History. Over time hundreds of artifacts belonging to the ship were removed from the bottom of Lake Champlain, but it is now impossible to determine their placement on the boat, how they came to be located exactly where they were, and other important factors. Nautical archaeology needs all these things to tell an accurate story of the wreck, but they had been lost when the ship was moved.

The gunboat *Philadelphia* is on display at the Museum of American History in Washington, D.C.

Schoolchildren who visit the Lake Champlain Maritime Museum today can see how frustrating this whole process can be. Each student is given a reproduction of an artifact found at the *Philadelphia* site and invited aboard the full-size replica *Philadelphia II* to determine where their mystery item was located and how it was used. Many of the items are easily identifiable—a kettle used for cooking, parts of the cannons, ammunition. One item that often confuses the students is a stone; it was used as ballast on the gunboat. Often the "captain" needs to show them where a collection of such stones is located under the officers' deck on the ship.

The exercise brings home to students the difficulty of determining the use of items found out of context. As the "captain" explains the techniques used in the removal of the *Philadelphia*, the students recognize the difficulty of reconstructing the gunboat from the fragmentary information that the 1935 dive provided.

The replica of the gunboat *Philadelphia*, named the *Philadelphia II*, is at the Lake Champlain Maritime Museum.

Students aboard the replica learn how historians reconstruct the past using artifacts and reenacting events.

The second Revolutionary War gunboat in Lake Champlain was the *Spitfire*. In 1997, an ongoing underwater mapping of the lakebed located it on the lake bottom. (The survey is being done before the wrecks are destroyed by zebra mussels.) The *Spitfire* is in perfect condition, with its mast still in place, as was that of the *Philadelphia*. Advances in equipment and diving technology have taken place in recent years, though, so her discovery has provided much more material for historians than the *Philadelphia*. She is being mapped and studied in place by divers wearing suits that allow them to study the ship close up, and to photograph and document every item at the site of the wreck. Items such as her ballast are easy to identify when seen in context. Each item of the ship lies where it fell when the ship sank. There is no immediate need to remove the ship from the lake, as it is not currently affected by the zebra mussels. The cold waters of the lake have kept her perfectly preserved for more than two hundred years, and there is time to reach a decision about what to do with the *Spitfire*. Should it be removed, changes in the technology of preservation of water-logged wood and metal objects would preserve the ship in much better condition than the *Philadelphia*. It is even possible that the *Spitfire* will be able to remain where she is.

The *Spitfire* also gives historians a chance to reinterpret what they learned from the *Philadelphia*. Because of the limitations of nautical archaeology of the 1930s, many of the conclusions regarding the gunboat's construction and role in the battle were based on guesswork. The replica, *Philadelphia II*, was built at the Lake Champlain Maritime Museum to test these guesses and has been used by reenactors attempting to re-create the lives of the men who would have served in Arnold's fleet.

In the short time since her discovery, the *Spitfire* has already provided exciting new historical information. Historians searched records trying to identify the ship exactly, and this led to the discovery of a historical document which "details the disposition of each of the seventeen vessels in the American naval force on Lake Champlain." Additional research about these gunboats and a study of this perfectly preserved artifact should provide much more information about the American Revolution on Lake Champlain.

The finding of the two ships casts light on the noteworthy technological changes in nautical archaeology over the last seventy years. Now, divers can study wrecks in shallow water in their location without disturbing their historical context. In addition, deep-sea research now uses robotic and manned submersibles; the *Titanic* and the Phoenician ships were found in this way. There is a multitude of historical material buried beneath water that covers two thirds of the planet. Now historians can use it to answer questions and fill in pieces of the historical puzzle long thought to be lost forever.

**Vessels such as the Johnson Sea Link Research Submersible are now being used for archaeological site documentation and recovery.**

# CHAPTER 5

# Lost City Found—The Story of Martin's Hundred

In 1607, 104 settlers from England arrived in Virginia and established the first permanent European colony in the future United States at Jamestown. Several years later, in 1618, a group of investors, the Society of Martin's Hundred (a hundred is the equivalent of a town), obtained a patent to establish a colony several miles from Jamestown. They sent off their first group of settlers (perhaps 140 in total) in 1619. William Harwood, the man appointed to lead the colony, arrived in Virginia in August 1620. Two years later, his colony lost more than half of its population in an attack by local Native Americans. Records give an account of the raid and massacre: "they basely and barbarously murthered [murdered], not sparing eyther [either] age or sexe, man, woman or childe; so sodaine [sudden] in their cruell execution, that few or none discerned the weapon or blow that brought them to destruction."

This is a representation of colonists in Virginia defending themselves against attack by Native Americans.

This group of settlers lost a reported seventy-eight members in this attack. Throughout the Virginia settlement a total of 347 people died. Historians estimate this represented about a quarter to a third of the residents. However, more than half of the people living at Martin's Hundred died. The remaining sixty-two people apparently abandoned the settlement and moved to Jamestown. A small group returned later and tried to reestablish the settlement. By 1625, only thirty people were living there. Over time the settlement disappeared and was essentially forgotten for more than three hundred years.

The location itself was a good one, and another house was built nearby in the 1730s. This was Carter's Grove Plantation, located farther up from the James River; the beautiful house, built on 500 acres (200 hectares), became part of Colonial Williamsburg in 1969. The process of planning for the U.S. Bicentennial, in 1976, led to the rediscovery of Martin's Hundred. Plans called for creating a new exhibit on the site to interpret colonial life. A required archaeological investigation was conducted to make sure that nothing of importance to the plantation's history was being disturbed by the project. Wrote the chief archaeologist of the project: "It must be rare, if not unique in . . . archaeology, for an excavation to be undertaken in the hope that nothing will be found, yet this was the reasoning."

The archaeologists did make a discovery, but it did not belong to the plantation's history. In fact, the findings obviously predated the plantation by a long time. Now the Colonial Williamsburg archaeologists had a mystery to solve—one that would lead to the discovery of artifacts and building remains older and more complete than anyone could have imagined.

At first the archaeologists knew only that the site predated the plantation. They guessed that they had found a small homestead from about 1650. But the artifacts that they began to find were from a period even earlier than that. Everything they found just increased their puzzlement. Nothing seemed to make sense. Wrote archaeologist Noël Hume of this "glumly obscure" site, "The more hard-to-date artifacts one finds . . . the greater the frustration—and the greater one's obligation to answer those questions."

However, the archeologists' frustration turned to excitement as they began to find evidence of a major settlement—a settlement with a puzzle. As the site was excavated, the post holes of every building (all that remained of them) showed evidence of

**Archaeologists excavated the land where buildings stood at part of the site that might be Martin's Hundred.**

Graves were uncovered at the excavation site. This male appeared to be a victim of foul play, judging from a gash above his right eye. Tobacco pipes found in his grave helped to date the skeleton to the early seventeenth century.

being burned. Then graves were found, including one showing evidence that the person had been murdered. A search of old records showed that much of the findings were consistent with the written accounts of the 1622 massacre.

They found items that provided a much better picture of life in the early days of American settlement than had ever been found before. They found glassware, pottery, and a great deal of evidence about everyday life. However they also found items that indicated that this was a site with major military implications—cannonballs, metal links from a mail shirt, and two helmets worn by soldiers at the time, which were the only "close" helmets found in the Americas. These are helmets that have a piece that closes over the wearer's face to protect it. Other items found indicated that a man of some wealth had lived here—broken window glass and the lead pieces that would have held that glass in place, silver and gold thread used only for the clothing of the wealthy, pieces of a fireplace insert, and tiles from a fireplace surround. This was obviously not just any homestead. It was the center of a settlement and perhaps the site of the home of the military governor.

Researching the few documents that exist from the time period helped to piece together the most complete story possible.

This is one of the "close" helmets that was found at the site that historians consider to be Martin's Hundred.

Here there was evidence of destruction and yet no evidence that the site had been repopulated. The excavations had found items that would only have been owned by the head of such a colony—there were, after all, strict laws that allowed only people of certain ranks to wear gold threads in their clothes. The records show that there was a cannon owned and located at Martin's Hundred. The well-educated guess of historians is that this was indeed Martin's Hundred.

Do we know for sure the story this site tells? No, we cannot. As archaeologist Noël Hume wrote: "An archaeologist has to reconstruct the past from a multitude of . . . fragments, and if he rejects all whose evidence is not irrefutable, rarely will he be able to draw a conclusion about anything . . . he must do the best he can with what he finds."

We do know that these are very early artifacts. They are remarkable for providing pieces of this jigsaw puzzle that tells us what life was like for the earliest English settlers in Virginia. This particular puzzle cannot be completed with the pieces at hand. That is, of course, exactly what makes history alive and always a great mystery story—an ongoing process of detection and reinterpretation.

## CHAPTER 6

# The Mythical Wall—
# The Great Wall of China

The Great Wall of China should be an easy historical artifact to document. It is 3,720 miles (5,990 km) long. It was built in the Ming dynasty. It is said to be the only man-made object that can be seen from space. What could be more valid than this wall? We know all we need to know. Or do we?

Let's start with one myth about the Great Wall—can the wall really be seen from the moon? Absolutely not! Cecil Adams, who maintains a website that "corrects" misinformation, quotes astronaut Alan Bean: "The only thing you can see from the moon is a beautiful sphere, mostly white . . . some blue . . . yellow . . . No man-made object is visible . . . In fact, when first leaving earth's orbit and only a few thousand miles away, no man-made object is visible at that point either."

**The Great Wall of China is not exactly what it seems to be. The myths that surround it have obscured the historic facts.**

The Great Wall *is* visible from a spaceship in orbit around the earth. But it is not the *only* man-made object so visible. Many man-made objects are visible from space, including any large-scale line on the earth's surface, such as complexes of roads, canals, and railroad lines.

A visitor to the actual wall does not see what the legend says it is. Historian Arthur Waldron writes that studying the reality of the Great Wall is difficult because of "the existence of a large body of misinformation and unreliable analysis found in the substantial popular literature . . . which continues to confuse scholars and ordinary people alike." The Great Wall, as substantial as it may sound, has a strong historic symbolism for the Chinese people. Basic facts about it are obscured by the myth.

China has a long history of wall building. Actually the history of wall building there is very similar to that of other civilizations. As humans began to evolve from hunter/gatherers to settled farmers, walls were built to fence off farming areas to protect their crops. The Chinese were early farmers and developed a series of walls to define agricultural spaces. The walls, as often happens, grew to define communities and then groups of communities. These simple earthen walls are sometimes counted as the beginning of the Great Wall.

There was an organized attempt to create a more continuous wall in China long before this was attempted anywhere else. Writer Leonard Fisher describes that decision this way, speaking as the emperor Ch'in Shih Huang Ti, who unified China about 2,200 years ago: "I shall . . . join all the walls together. I shall have one long wall across the top of China . . . It will be six horses wide at the top, eight at the bottom, and five men high." Fisher says that this project involved a million people and took ten years to complete. Many people claim that this is the same Great Wall that survives today. But archaeological evidence shows that what is known as the Great Wall today is not even located in the same place as this section of wall built in 221 B.C.

Peter Hessler has recently returned from driving the entire length of the Great Wall, an expedition he reported for *National Geographic* magazine. He summarizes the difficulty of documenting the Great Wall this way: "In the popular consciousness, the Great Wall is a unified concept, but in fact northern China is criss-crossed by many different walls built by many different dynasties . . . the Great Wall's supposed characteristics—that it is continuous, that the entire structure is over 2,000 years old . . . are false."

Historian Jonathan Fryer would agree. He states that the wall is "a conglomeration of barriers built at different times for different reasons, and little of what we can see today is the same fortification as that built by the First Emperor." He also notes that the importance of the Great Wall lies in the fact that it "is the paramount symbol of China's standing and achievement." This symbolism is what makes documenting the Great Wall such a controversial task for historians.

The wall that tourists visit today actually dates from the

Ming dynasty in the 1500s. It began as an earthen wall to help keep the invading Mongols from the city of Beijing. Over the years the wall was strengthened and maintained as a defensive barrier. The oldest sections of the wall are "a kind of adobe made from soil, straw, tamarisk, egg yolk and rice paste . . . no one can repair it. 'We no longer know how,'" writes one researcher. Other, more modern sections are made of fired brick or stone, but all are deteriorating. (An international group has been formed to raise funds to preserve the wall.) What we call the Great Wall today is made up of these collapsing wall sections.

Even at its best, it was never the all-encompassing wall of myth. Certain areas, especially around Beijing, did develop into complete fortifications. But this was only part of the wall. How long this wall ever was is still disputed today. Historian Waldron writes of attempting to get an accurate statement of the wall's length and encountering numbers ranging from 1,600 miles (2,575 kilometers) to 31,000 miles (49,910 km). Waldron also notes that until modern times the Chinese language did not contain a character conveying the concept of an all-encompassing "great wall." He states: "If an ancient Great Wall had existed, it almost certainly would have had a single fixed name . . . used consistently." Instead different names were used to refer to it over time, unlike other "ancient" sites such as temples or rivers.

The story of the Great Wall and its significance today illustrates one of the great problems that historians encounter in trying to interpret the past. Sometimes what a people or nation "remembers" as important about its past is simply not true. The Chinese would like to believe that the Great Wall dates back to 221 B.C., making it a marvelous symbol of the engineering ability of their ancestors. The real stuff of history—the documents and the archaeology—does not support this conviction. The ruins known today as the Great Wall are only five hundred or so years old. They are still marvelous, but they are not what the myth suggests they are.

## CHAPTER 7

# The People Before the Europeans Came

**M**any schools teach the history of the Americas as beginning with the arrival of Columbus in 1492. However, one historian notes, "the European settlement of the Americas, for all its modern political significance, is just a late phase of the history of man on the American continent." The Spanish explorers of the 1500s found two civilizations in the Americas—civilizations that rivaled any in the world at the time of European exploration and "discovery" of the New World—that of the Aztecs, in Mexico, and that of the Incas in the Andes mountains of Peru. There were also great ruins of earlier civilizations, such as the Maya in the Yucatán Peninsula. The Europeans did not come to a wilderness or a primitive undeveloped region.

The Aztecs were a people with a well-developed civilization; they kept written records of their history and developed large cities, including Tenochtitlán with three hundred thousand residents. They built transportation and communication networks that were advanced for their time and created beautiful works of art and architecture. In no way could they have been deemed inferior to their European counterparts.

The Aztecs were defeated and destroyed by the Spanish conquistadors under Hernando Cortés in 1520. In fact, Cortés himself "declared that Tenochtitlán was the size of Seville or Córdoba . . . In size, basic pattern, and magnificence, Tenochtitlán reminded many of the conquistadors of the major cities of Spain." The Aztecs "lived in independent tribal . . . groups and created a religious art and architecture without rival in the Americas." The Franciscan and Dominican priests who worked with the people recorded their culture, their art, their language. However, all this knowledge would be deliberately forgotten for a long time.

When the Spanish arrived in 1519, they were seeking valuable minerals, notably silver and gold. They quickly defeated the Aztecs, who would not provide them with what they sought. The

This is a depiction of what Tenochtitlán might have looked like in the sixteenth century.

Spanish failed to understand that the quantities of silver and gold that they expected to find simply did not exist. Military losses of the Aztecs combined with disease that was brought to them by the Spanish. Smallpox killed a high proportion of the native population; some sources indicate as high as 95 percent.

The Aztecs had been a conquering people themselves. By the 1400s they had incorporated a rival civilization—the Mayans, who lived in southern Mexico and Central America—into their empire. The Mayans were noted for their ritual observances and the beautiful temples they built. They had a written language of pictorial symbols—hieroglyphs—similar to what the Egyptians had used. They had developed their own calendar and were experts in astronomy.

The Aztecs had also conquered and incorporated the Toltecs and several other smaller tribal groups around A.D. 1200. One historian notes: "They consciously absorbed from their neighbors the skills and knowledge of their predecessors."

Just as they had previously assimilated other cultures into their own, the Aztec survivors were assimilated into the new Spanish culture. Cortés could write of Tlaxcala, an Aztec city: "Its houses are as fine . . . [as] those of Granada. . . . Its provisions and food are likewise very superior. . . . Nothing is lacking . . . utensils, garments, footwear . . . gold, silver and precious stones . . . ornaments made of feathers . . . earthenware of many kinds and excellent quality . . . Wood, charcoal, medicinal and sweet smelling herbs . . . public baths." However, over the next hundred years the Aztec language and customs evolved into one that blended with that of their European conquerors. Unfortunately for the Aztecs, all the marvels recorded by the first Spanish arrivals were no longer mentioned. Instead they were characterized as primitive people who had practiced shocking rituals of human sacrifice in the past.

An official Spanish royal policy was established, supposedly to protect their interests. The king ordered the leaders of the colony "to instruct the natives in the faith [Catholicism] and the way of life consonant with it, until the Indians reached full cultural maturity, as measured by Spanish norms." This policy of teaching the native peoples to be Spanish rapidly turned them into the primitives that the Spanish government saw them to be. When the Aztecs were deprived of their language and culture, their glorious past was totally forgotten within a hundred years. Some modern researchers have even found it impossible to accept that the ancestors of the people living in the region today could have created the wonders now being discovered by archaeology.

Only in recent years have historians begun to reinterpret the Aztec past. Archaeologists have led the way with excavations that have revealed the Aztecs' technical capabilities in art and architecture. In the words of one researcher, speaking of the excavations of the Aztec Templo Mayor, which began in 1978, "The ritual heart of the Aztec empire . . . has been revealed for the first time." These finds have mandated a total rethinking of Aztec history in the pre-Columbian period. A different picture of the Aztec past is emerging. The rediscovery of Tenochtitlán, the

This is part of the ruins of Templo Mayor that presented historians with an entirely new picture of the Aztec past.

Aztec ritual skulls that were found in the ruins reveal that Templo Mayor was the ceremonial center of the Aztec city of Tenochtitlán.

An anthropology researcher examines the remains of the Aztec ritual skulls in order to gain information about their lifestyle.

Archaeologists examine the site at Templo Mayor where one of fourteen stone carvings was found in 2005. The discovery is part of an ongoing project that has been investigating pre-Hispanic cultures in Mexico City.

Aztec capital city, has "brought to light vast amounts of data on the life, customs, and achievements of the Aztecs." Found in the excavations were "ceramics, stonework, sculpture, architecture, painting," writes one researcher, who says that the Aztecs were a society "equally able to conquer distant regions and write poetry expressing . . . profound feelings."

In the Andes mountains of Peru a second large civilization was conquered by the Spanish, in 1532. The Inca had ruled a vast empire in South America since about A.D. 1200. The Inca did not have a written history. However, their engineering skills were exceptional. Their empire was connected by a large network of roads and suspension bridges, some of which are still used today. They created beautiful buildings, including a wonderful mountain palace at Machu Picchu. One historian records that the Inca were "highly skilled stoneworkers, able to construct buildings of massive stone so well fitted together that a knife blade will not squeeze between them." These mortarless buildings give us a wonderful chance to study their abilities.

**Machu Picchu is solid proof that the Inca had extraordinary engineering skills.**

The Inca people were also expert crafters known for fine silver and gold work and textiles. Many of their colorful and intricately woven textiles remain today, covering the mummies that they carefully prepared for the afterlife. They had, in addition, a sophisticated system of government that allowed those they conquered a greater degree of democracy at the local level than was common at the time. Historians note that this combination of "territorial expansion," some level of conquered territorial self-governance, and a role in their new empire, was "unique in American annals."

Religious ceremonies were an important part of the Incan culture. In addition, learning was prized, and the Inca had a sophisticated knowledge of astronomy and mathematics. As with the Aztecs, the Spaniards found a society which equaled theirs in culture and learning, but could not match them militarily. The

Inca were conquered by Francisco Pizarro in 1532 in one battle; the Incan leader, Atahuallpa, was executed.

As with the Aztecs, history was written by the winners and the Inca were portrayed as a primitive people. It is interesting to note that "Inca" was not even what they called themselves. The word refers to their aristocracy, "a very privileged class of people who claimed their divine origin from the Sun." The Spanish mistakenly applied it to the entire society. Only now, recent excavations and study of their cultural rituals, especially their mummification of the dead, have forced historians to reinterpret the Inca past. Because they had no written language, their artifacts and evidence of their engineering and scientific skills point the way for this new picture of the richness of their culture to emerge. Writes one researcher, theirs "is a story written with a lexicon of images, a vocabulary of stones that tells of an extraordinary social, military, and religious organization."

The Aztecs and the Inca are prime examples of how peoples can be written out of the historical record when they are conquered by another nation. The pieces that were needed to create a picture of their past are either unnoticed or emerge only slowly over time. Fortunately for both of these civilizations, enough physical evidence exists to allow modern historians to reinterpret their story and complete the puzzle in a way that reclaims their rightful place in history.

## CHAPTER 8

# And Then They Were Gone— The Story of Mesa Verde

Carved into the side of a mesa in southwestern Colorado is a series of adobe villages called Mesa Verde. They were obviously built to last; just as obviously, they were deserted long before they needed to be. These ruins embody an intriguing historical mystery in the United States. They are all the more intriguing because many think that the solution to this mystery may help us deal with some modern urban problems.

Every year thousands of people visit the beautiful cliff dwellings that the people of Mesa Verde constructed with great care, lived in, and then abandoned. Some of these ruins are spectacular groupings of dwellings of up to two hundred rooms built into the face of the cliffs. The people who occupied these dwellings are often referred to as the Anasazi, although they are now usually called the Ancestral Puebloans. This new name rec-

ognizes that although they left their cliff homes, they themselves did not disappear. Their descendants are alive today, represented by the many native Pueblo peoples in the Southwest.

Historians estimate that several thousand people lived in the cliff dwellings at Mesa Verde and at other sites such as Chaco Canyon, in New Mexico, and Canyon de Chelly, in Arizona. The first large pueblo, or communal dwelling, is thought to date from about A.D. 900. Historians estimate all of the pueblos were abandoned by 1300. The people who lived there left us many mysteries.

Why did they build into the sides of this mesa originally? Historians' best guess is that "the cliff dwellings provided an uncommon measure of security for their inhabitants." Others theorize that weather was a factor, or possibly religion. The cliff dwellings took a great deal of labor to build—labor that seems excessive for homes that were only occupied for a few hundred years. As one researcher notes: "The people had to gather stones along the canyon slope, carry dirt and water to make mortar and fashion their house arrangements according to the contour of the alcoves. The people had to carry everything they needed . . . over rough terrain."

Some believe that people lived in the cliff dwellings for religious reasons, and note that the people were crowded into small living spaces because "they devoted what seems to be a disproportionately large share of the space to their kivas [religious buildings]." Another researcher writes, "The time and effort that went into the construction of a great kiva is an indication of the importance of the ceremonies conducted in them." He also comments on the contents of the kiva, from "ceremonial pottery shapes" to "petroglyphs and pictographs [that] . . . appear to portray supernatural beings."

The Ancestral Puebloans' engineering feats were spectacular. A system of roads connected the various settlements of the region. Water had to be collected for use on the site; dams and

Until recently, little has been known about how Anasazi pottery was made. Artists and archaeologists have been working together to gain insight into Anasazi production methods so that historians can learn more about their lives.

reservoirs were built for both drinking water and irrigation. These were the first "big" cities on U.S. soil. Historian Gene Stewart speaks of the settlements as "the highest cultural development and the most concentrated move towards urbanism [city dwelling]." Another historian, Jesse Fewkes, notes that the information with which to study their culture is limited: "The most reliable data we now have to aid us in interpreting their culture are their buildings and archaeological remains. . . . Their houses are the most significant."

Many believe that another mystery about these Ancestral Puebloans is related to the concentration of people in their communities. The cliff dwellings were abandoned far too soon. There is no evidence that it was for military reasons—no sign of attack or disastrous fire or other calamity. Again there is speculation about the reason for this departure. The people did not leave the area—their descendants still reside there today. If they were not driven out, why did they go? Their history shows that after they left their cliff dwellings they chose to live in smaller communities. This leads many to theorize that ecological and environmental pressures caused them to leave their mesa homes. Perhaps drought overtook their agricultural and water needs. Perhaps, as some suspect, "the inevitable stresses and social unrest" caused by the crowded living conditions led them to disperse and seek simpler lives on a smaller social scale. Notes one researcher, "the most plausible explanation for deserting Mesa Verde lies in the final culmination of a problem the Anasazi had long been aware of . . . steady depletion of resources accompanying lengthy occupation . . . worsened by one of the droughts that cyclically occurred. . . . In small disheartened groups they gradually filtered away."

The site at Mesa Verde and its artifacts seem as if they would provide more than enough information to find the "right" answers. The site is fairly recent. The artifacts are strong and the descendents of these very same people still live in the area. And yet, the answers seem elusive. This mystery should be easier to solve than it is. The only answers that historians can find that seem to fit the facts of the site and its artifacts indicate that environmental issues may have doomed the city. This historical mystery may yet hold answers for the crowded, water-dependent Western cities of today.

The possible connection to our world today makes this puzzle so interesting. The belief that history is fixed and unchanging often leads to a feeling that there is little we need to know about the past. Since history has moved on, and technological change has been so great, it can seem that historical events are merely curiosities to be studied. However, many historians believe that we need to understand the past not simply because it is interesting to know, but also because it may hold the answer to some of the challenges we face today. Some of the issues that were either solved then or left unsolved because no answer could be found are ones that still trouble us today. These historians believe in the old saying: "Those who cannot remember the past are condemned to repeat it." They see here a historical puzzle for which we need to find the solution.

## CHAPTER 9

# Proving That Some "Myths" Are True—The Vikings at L'Anse aux Meadows

The first Europeans to walk on the soil of the New World were Christopher Columbus and his crew, in 1492. Columbus had "discovered" North America. He had not even known that there was a continent here. He thought he was sailing to India. That is the history taught in schools for ages.

But the truth of the matter is that Columbus did not discover North America. People had been living here for thousands of years, developing their own cultures quite well without European involvement. And was Columbus even the first European to discover North America? No. This land had been discovered and actually settled for a short time by a group of Vikings almost five hundred years before Columbus and his men arrived. In 1960 the Viking site, located on the tip of Newfoundland, Canada, at L'Anse aux Meadows, was found, and with it were found wonderful artifacts that documented this first European settlement in the New World.

A visitor to a museum exhibit depicting the unbelievable ocean journeys of the Vikings may be most amazed that anyone would be brave—or foolhardy—enough to travel in their ships. Viking ships were made of planks of oak or pine, called strakes, that were riveted together in an overlap pattern to keep out water. Oceangoing boats had two extra planks, to allow for waves. The ships could be rowed or sailed. The sails were of wool woven into long strips that were sewn together and then coated with animal fat for waterproofing. The rigging for the sails was woven of horsehair or rope made from walrus hide. The ships carried thirty to a hundred men. The colorful shields of the Vikings were stored inside the ships and were used to protect the oar holes during battles. Researchers noted that "The Viking expansion . . . was possible first and foremost because of superb shipbuilding." Modern replicas have proven the boats seaworthy.

The Viking discovery of North America should be easy to document. Oral accounts of the settlement had existed since the days of settlement. The Vikings who took part in the discovery

Researchers have built and sailed replicas of Viking ships to learn more about Viking culture. This replica showed that Viking ships were effective vessels.

of Vinland were real, verified, historical persons, and parts of their stories had been documented for some time. But the most important part of this story was missing—history had lost the site of settlement. Vinland existed in the Norse sagas (historical stories) but could not be placed on any map. Without knowing the site to prove the sagas real, people over the years had come to see them as legends, rather than as fact. Columbus's discovery of America five hundred years later was the exploration that appeared in history books.

The Norse sagas, which were written down probably around A.D. 1200, tell of the gradual Viking expansion from Norway into Iceland around the year A.D. 930. They tell also of Eirik or Erik Thorvaldsson, known to history as Erik the Red. Exiled from Iceland because he "had slain one too many enemies. . . . Erik assembled ships and followers and cast off into the western sea." He located Greenland and founded a settlement there. The sagas tell of a trading vessel that loses its way returning to Greenland from Iceland and sees land west of the Greenland site. The ship corrects its course and arrives safely, and no immediate visit to this new land is made.

Erik's son, Leif Eriksson, known as Leif the Lucky, travels west with a group of about thirty-five settlers around the year A.D. 1000 searching for new land. He lands there and settlers build houses and winter at the site, which they called Vinland. They return to Greenland the following year. Later another expedition travels back to the same site and lives in the houses there for two years before returning to Greenland. Yet another expedition also visits the site and stays for another two years. Finally, an expedition led by Erik the Red's daughter visits the site and spends another year there. Another saga records fewer actual expeditions to the site, but has larger groups living there.

Many historians had long been searching to find the site of Vinland. Researchers trying to find Vinland had access to two old maps from the early 1600s, in addition to the sagas. One of the maps was drawn by a man who claimed to be using information from the 1200s. Thus the maps represented material that should have been accurate based on the accounts of the day. With the knowledge of the sagas and the maps, researchers should have been able to find the site.

One confusing piece of information, however, stymied all searchers for years. The sagas reported that the settlers had seen wheat and grapes. Speculation went on for years as to where grapes might have been seen. If the settlement was called Vinland because of its grapes, then the maps must be inaccurate, because wild grapes only grow as far north as New England. Many argued for a New England location; and, for a while, one group of historians believed that Vinland was a site in Rhode Island. Then an analysis of ruins found there set forth an estimated date of 1600—six hundred years too late.

It may have taken so long to locate the site because of a translation error of the word *Vinland.* Helge Ingstad, the Norwegian explorer who finally located Vinland, looked beyond the accepted translation and explored a new possibility. He believed that Vinland was so named not because of vines, but from the Norse term for meadows. After exploring Greenland, he turned his efforts to Newfoundland. He noted that the Vikings were regularly traveling and trading back and forth from Greenland to Norway, a distance of 1,500 miles (2,400 km). Traveling another 250 miles (400 km) to find better land for a settlement was a natural extension of the exploring they had already done. Greenland had a harsh climate, and the people living there were determined to find a location that would better suit their work.

It was autumn when Ingstad located an area that he thought matched the description in the sagas, what he calls "a great plain with green meadows." Landing his boat, he found a small village of fishers living in the town of L'Anse aux Meadows. He asked whether there were any old ruins in the area, and he was led to a bay where he found some overgrown mounds. Ingstad wrote: "It was almost *déjà-vu,* so much was reminiscent of what I had seen in the Norse settlements of Greenland."

These sod houses at L'Anse aux Meadows are replicas that were built in honor of the Vikings that settled there.

Ingstad organized a series of seven archaeological expeditions to explore the site, from 1961 to 1968. The digs found eight house sites, and within them features characteristic of other known Viking settlements in Greenland and elsewhere. There was a typical Norse hearth and ember pit, a spindle used by the women for spinning wool, and stone lamps identical to those found in sites in Iceland. There was a blacksmith's workshop

This is a reconstruction of the interior of the sod home at L'Anse aux Meadows. This was built to obtain a better understanding of the Vikings' lifestyle more than a thousand years ago.

with a large stone anvil, and pieces of iron fragments and slag around it. The radiocarbon dating of the site confirmed that the items found were from the time period when the sagas spoke of the settlements at Vinland—about A.D. 1000.

The archaeological evidence does not provide an explanation for why the Vikings abandoned this site and returned to Greenland. These people were more than just good explorers—they were farmers, hunters, and fishers attempting to find a permanent location to begin a new life. They traveled with their wives. At least one child was born at the site in L'Anse aux Meadows.

The site at L'Anse aux Meadows became more of a camp for exploring the area than a permanent settlement. One historian notes it was a "base" for further exploration of "lumber, butternuts, and, presumably, the grapes brought back . . . and stored over the winter to be taken back to Greenland." He goes on to theorize that Vinland was actually a huge area with L'Anse aux Meadows as "the base from which it was explored." Within a short time, perhaps a few decades, the Vikings retreated back to Greenland. Eventually, even those settlements were abandoned. Ultimately, it was not distances from Greenland that caused the Vikings to abandon the settlement. It was instead the native people they found living there, the Beothuks peoples (extinct since about 1800), whom they called the Skraelings. (The sagas detail increasingly difficult problems with the native peoples who wanted the new arrivals to provide them with weapons.)

The mystery had been solved—Vinland had been found, and history as it is taught from now on cannot claim that the first Europeans to reach North America were Christopher Columbus and his crew. Instead, the first visitors had come about five hundred years earlier, had settled for a number of years, and then left because "the distances back home were too great, the populations too small, the natives too belligerent." But the traces they had left behind, combined with their sagas and maps, had provided historians with enough pieces of their historical puzzle so they would eventually be found.

# CHAPTER 10

# The Distance Between Myth and Reality— Who Was King Arthur?

King Arthur was the supposed British king who defeated the Saxons, organized the country, and brought peace to Britain during the Dark Ages in the sixth century. He carried a magic sword called Excalibur with a sheath that could heal any injuries. His advisers included a magician, Merlin, who was his teacher. He created the Round Table—the table of King Arthur and his knights—and led his country wisely, guided by the Code of Chivalry. He was ultimately defeated by treachery from within his own group of knights. Dying, he was transported to the Isle of Avalon, with a promise from Merlin that he would return in England's hour of greatest need. This is a story of "the greatest figure in the folklore of Britain . . . a man at the forefront of the Britons' heroic defence of their homeland and heritage." It is a story of heroism and courage, a story filled with romance and drama. And some of it just might be true.

This is a depiction of King Arthur's mythic Round Table, showing him at the head of the table surrounded by his noble knights.

The story of King Arthur dates back to a time in Great
Britain when record keeping was unreliable. King Arthur is said
to have lived in the fifth or sixth century. Most of what we know
about him comes from the writings of Geoffrey of Monmouth,
several hundred years after Arthur's time. Geoffrey claimed that
his information came from a book he had seen—a book that
does not exist today. Geoffrey's tales of Arthur became the basis
for a series of stories that together comprise what is now called
the Arthurian legends. Over the years, these have been developed
into a large body of tales that, taken together, seem to provide a
plausible history of England at the time after the Romans abandoned England, their northernmost colony, but before a documented history is available.

The tale told by Geoffrey of Monmouth is that of a war
leader, or perhaps a king, who arises and unites the local kings in
a fight to stop the continuing attacks of the Saxons on English
soil. Arthur leads his armies in several battles in which the Sax-

ons are defeated and then tries to keep the country united in peacetime. Eventually events force him into one last battle, perhaps because of the betrayal by his own son and the desertion of his best knight, Lancelot. In that battle Arthur is mortally wounded. Upon these spare facts, the legend has grown over time to encompass a Round Table, a search for the Holy Grail, and a whole series of chivalric tales of knights fighting for noble ends. In the words of one historian, "Much of the widespread skepticism about the historicity of Arthur stems from the undoubted fact that his name became attached to unhistorical tales, to fabulous wonders, and to places which can never have been connected with him."

There is no doubt of the magic that the Arthurian legends bring to the history of Britain. There is also no doubt that the legends of Arthur have grown in part because they came to represent a simpler, more gallant time; and they offer, in Merlin's prophecy, the promise that this spirit will return to Britain. The legends have their own complex history—of kings using Arthur to justify their own kingship, of artifacts being created (a Round Table was created in the 1200s)—which say more about their own time period than that of Arthur. So how can historians sort through the legends, review the information found in Geoffrey of Monmouth's writings of around A.D. 1100, and determine why this legend began in the first place? How do we find fact in the midst of what one researcher calls "pseudohistory"?

Historian Leslie Alcock approaches the problem by returning to the documentation that exists for the Dark Ages. Contained in a group of early written documents known as the *British Historical Miscellany* are the Easter Annals (also called the Annales Cambriae), which are listings of important events from the time period A.D. 447 to 954 (although historians believe some of the earlier events were added later). The Easter Annals contain two references to Arthur. One names him as leader in a battle at Badon; the other refers to his death at Camlann. Neither of these sites appears on the map of Great Britain today, but most historians accept their location as being in the area near Glastonbury. The two events are twenty-three years apart in the Annals and, according to Alcock, "assure us that Arthur was an authentic person; one important enough to be deemed worthy of an entry in an Easter Annal; most probably a king or prince, but if not that, then emphatically a great warrior." But how do we know that these entries are accurate and not just legend? Alcock documented that every other name mentioned in the Easter Annals is that of a person who can be confirmed historically. Thus the logical assumption is that Arthur also is historical, since there would be no reason for him to be the only person mentioned in the Annals who is not.

Geoffrey Ashe takes a different approach to the problem of identifying Arthur. He believes that we would not have the stories from Geoffrey of Monmouth if Arthur did not exist. He researches the Dark Ages on the theory that Arthur is there, but perhaps not under that name. He wants to find out who did the deeds now associated with Arthur's name, such as defeating the Saxons. In the correct time period he finds a Roman Briton who matches many of the achievements attributed to Arthur. He finds a general who signs a letter as Riothamus. Ashe translates that "name" and concludes that Riothamus in Latin is a title, not a personal name; a title, more importantly, that translates as High King. Ashe decides that perhaps this is Arthur, and that he signed his official documents by title rather than by personal name, which would have been Artorius in Latin. He concludes: "In the High King called Riothamus we have, at last, a documented person as the starting point of the legend. He is the only such person on record who does anything Arthurian . . . he is the only one to whom any large part of the story can be related."

While these historians have turned to the written record to try to prove that Arthur was indeed a historical person, others have moved on to the historic sites named in the legend in an attempt to find documentation there. Archaeological digs at Tintagel, where Arthur is supposed to have been born, and Cadbury,

The ruins at Tintagel Castle revealed artifacts that were dated back to the fifth or sixth century, the time of Arthur's legend.

which may be the site of the famed Camelot, have provided some evidence that can document at least part of the story. Archaeologist C. A. Ralegh Radford excavated at Tintagel expecting to find only materials dating from the eleventh century or later. Instead, pottery was found that could be dated back to the fifth or sixth century, indicating that this site was occupied at the time of the legendary Arthur. On Glastonbury Tor, the hill long associated in the legend with Avalon, building remains were found in the 1960s by archaeologist Philip Rahtz dating to the correct time period. Excavations at Cadbury revealed more ruins of the time period: "the foundations of a fair-sized hall came to light. It had been timber-built, with skilled workmanship . . . someone with great resources of manpower reoccupied the vacant hill and renewed its defenses on a grandiose scale."

None of this research, of course, can answer the question exactly—we still do not know if there was ever a king or war leader of Britain in the sixth century named Arthur who defeated the Sax-

In 1966 archaeologists excavated the ruins of Cadbury Castle. Archaeologist Sir Mortimer Wheeler claimed that he was "almost certain" that Camelot had been discovered.

ons and was later defeated by treachery. What we do have are enough pieces of the puzzle for historians to determine that the story is more than a myth. There was indeed a person who served as the basis for the legends of Arthur. Was his name actually Arthur? Is he Riothamus, the High King? We do not have the answers to these questions. Whether we ever will depends on what pieces of the puzzle historians and archaeologists find in the future.

CHAPTER 11

# What Happened When the City Moved?—Italica, the Forgotten Roman City

Archaeologists are often frustrated by the fact that some of the best ruins, those that they most desire to excavate and explore, are hidden under layers of development. Most major archaeological sites are located in places that have remained occupied through historic time. This means that old sites were often torn apart by people who came to use the ruins as building materials for their own projects. This is especially true (and especially frustrating) in regard to Roman sites. All that good stone, worked into evenly shaped blocks by the Romans, found new use over the years. As a result, Roman sites are rarely found in any complete form. It is the archaeologist's dream to have a pristine site to work with—a dream that seldom comes true.

Roman sites can vary greatly from one location to the next. Ruins may be as fragmentary as the few stones marking the site

The ruins of an ancient Roman amphitheater at Arles in southern France

of Segontium, in northern Wales, or as complete as the wonderful aqueduct at Segovia, Spain, which is still supplying water to the old walled city. The Romans chose the sites where they built their cities well, and most ruins are located in settlements that have been continuously occupied. Thus it is no surprise that a Roman street was found beneath the footings of Notre Dame Cathedral, in the city of Paris, or that major Roman ruins can be found in the cities of southern France, like Nimes and Arles. The older the city in the area formerly under the control of Rome, the more likely it seems to be that the old city is built on the ruins of that Roman occupation.

One exception lies near Seville, Spain, and raises interesting questions that archaeologists are now working with. The Roman colonies in Spain (called Hispania by the Romans) were among the most prosperous in the empire. The large Roman colonies at Tarraco (Tarragona) and Augusta Emerita (Mérida) provide extensive ruins to explore. But the visitor searching Italica for

Rome's oldest colony in Spain faces quite a journey. This is not a regular stop on the tourist itinerary, even though it lies less than 10 miles (16 km) from Seville, the ancient capital of the Andalusia region and a popular tourist destination. It is almost impossible to find information about how to visit the site, which is near the modern town of Santiponce. The site itself is not well marked. American tourists who do locate it will not find many other visitors and rarely anyone who speaks a language other than Spanish. But, when found, Italica houses an amazing secret.

There have actually been two Italicas. The original is one of the oldest Roman colonies anywhere, founded around 206 B.C. by Scipio Africanus after his victory over the Carthaginians. Other colonies in Spain would become larger and more prosperous, but Italica would give Rome two of her greatest emperors—Trajan and Hadrian. It was Hadrian who, visiting the city of his birth, decided to create "an entirely new town" north of the earlier settlement. His vision of the town was one whose "enormous public buildings, wide streets and richly decorated houses represent the urban ideal." Hadrian left his architectural mark all over his empire, from the defensive wall in Britain named for him to the villa outside of Rome that still attracts tourists. Here in Spain he chose to build a model city—it was to be a home for wealthy citizens who could afford to build large houses sited on broad streets of stone. It had its own theater and an amphitheater "important enough a monument in its own right, being the largest in the Peninsula and the fourth largest in the Roman world."

The remains of the original older city at Italica disappeared over time, buried under the modern suburb of Seville called Santiponce. Hadrian's new city would hide its treasures for archaeologists of the future. It is available to us now because those designing the city made a critical error. They disregarded the fact that the soils here would not support the large homes being built in the new city. "Walls began to settle and structures subsided," records one historian, S. J. Keay. "Within a generation the mansions, baths and the new forum were all abandoned."

This abandonment of Italica makes it a wonderful site for archaeologists today. It was "deserted after the Roman period, leaving [its] ruins intact and accessible to modern excavation," according to historian Leonard Curchin. Unlike other "more successful" Roman sites whose Roman presence "have been destroyed, buried or remodeled" and whose "exploration is impeded by modern occupation," this one is pristine.

Historians have access here to a frozen moment in time, occupied for less than a generation and not corrupted by later changes. The mosaic floors in the "sumptuous and elegant" homes are perfectly preserved. Archaeologists are more used to excavations like those taking place in Tarragona, Spain, where the remains of the Circus (the Roman chariot track) form one of the walls of several restaurants, supermarkets, and stores. At Tarragona, historians deal with "the massacred remains of the only

The ruins of the Roman amphitheater at Italica are in perfect condition for archaeologists to study and learn a great deal about the lives of the ancient Romans. At the center of the arena is a great pit (shown above), which was used for gladiators and events with wild animals.

The intricate mosaic floors at Italica have been well preserved. The floors were specially designed to reflect the purpose of some of the buildings.

known Roman theatre in Catalonia . . . a sharp reminder of the problems inherent in the preservation of our archaeological heritage in urban areas."

A visitor to Italica will be quite impressed to see the actual work of analyzing history in process. Very little of the city has yet been excavated. The excavation of the amphitheater is complete, but little has been done in the rest of the site. Notes a brochure: "In the city there were thought to have been, as far as we know, six public buildings and some fifty houses . . . the major part of which have not been excavated." As the visitor stands and walks along the roads looking at the grassy mounds that mark the remains of buildings, there is a very real sense that this site provides a unique opportunity to expand our knowledge of life in one of the most important provinces of ancient Rome. The few excavated blocks reveal enviable mosaics. What lies beneath the unexcavated mounds? What wonders? What story will the ruins tell?

Italica holds a unique place in archaeological history simply because it was not spoiled by later human occupation like most other sites in the Roman world. Now, when we have the means to study and understand these ruins, historians have the ideal site to interpret this time and place. Who knows how the stories found here will change what we know about Roman life? Who knows what pieces of the historical puzzle have laid buried here for millennia, still waiting to be found?

We can hope that the puzzle pieces buried here will tell the story of Italica. It is important to note that puzzle pieces for other stories around the world are also being found. Right now there are "lost" cities being studied throughout the world. Loulan, an ancient Chinese city that was important to the silk trade two thousand years ago, is being researched intensively. A new find of a settlement in Ecuador may provide evidence that humans reached the upper part of the Amazon River 4,500 years ago, much earlier than had been thought. The Archaeological Society of India recently announced the discovery of Buddhist treasures possibly dating back to the 400s at a monastery excavation. Historians, archaeologists, and anthropologists are all hunting to find the answers.

At Italica there are no guidebooks, no gift shops, no mobs of tourists. This is an actual workshop for studying life almost two thousand years ago. Here, as the archaeologists carry out excavations that will continue for decades, is a place where the process of making history and collecting the pieces of the puzzle are happening today. Who knows what historical magic the research will turn up.

## CHAPTER 12

# Buried History—The Story of Herculaneum and Pompeii

I t is one of the best-documented natural disasters of the first millennium. Powerful eyewitness accounts of Pliny the Younger, based on his own observations and those of his uncle, Pliny the Elder, vividly describe the eruption of Mount Vesuvius on August 24, A.D. 79. He tells of the "black and dreadful cloud bursting out in gusts of igneous serpentine vapour . . . long fantastic flames, resembling flashes of lightning but much larger." The Roman town of Pompeii was buried in ash and pumice by the eruption. All that could be seen were the tops of the tallest buildings. Ten miles (16 km) away, Herculaneum suffered a similar fate, abruptly catching its citizens at lunchtime. Food was left in place on the tables, as people fled the thick pyroclastic flow that destroyed the city. The eruption of Vesuvius was estimated by one scientist to be "ten times the size of Mt. St. Helens in 1980."

After the eruption, both cities simply disappeared from the historical record. In the 1500s, during the Renaissance, there was a revival of interest in the classical world of the Greeks and Romans, and an attempt was made to discover the buried cities. Pompeii was actually found when a channel was dug to bring water from a river to a villa, and the "tunnel cut right through the hidden ruins." However, the find was not recognized, and the city slept on for another 150 years. In the 1700s the two cities were found again. At first, excavations could not be done at Herculaneum because the pyroclastic flow that buried the city had hardened into a solid rock matrix that was almost impossible to remove. At Pompeii digging was easier, but what was done there cannot really be called archaeology. It was more like treasure hunting, and no one knows now how much information was lost in these haphazard digs.

When modern scientific archaeological excavations began at Pompeii, no one was prepared for what would be found. Archaeologists discovered unexplainable holes in the ash and pumice layer. Someone had the idea of filling one of the cavities with plaster to see what shape would emerge. When the hardened plaster was dug out of the surrounding lava, there was a shocking discovery—the cavities in the ash were formed by the bodies of those who had suffocated to death while trying to escape the

This is one of the plaster casts that was made from a person who died at Pompeii during the eruption of Mount Vesuvius.

city. The bodies themselves had disintegrated long ago. A collection of these plaster casts of the bodies is kept at Pompeii and at nearby archaeological museums. Even though the casts only record the space occupied by the living person in a general way, there is enough detail to show that they died a gruesome and horrible death. It is a powerful sight to see the young girl lying face down on the ground, her face buried in her hands; the man crouched into a ball trying to avoid the ash and fumes; even a poor dog trying to break his chain to run away from the devastating eruption.

Of course, beautiful things were also found at Pompeii. Statues and plenty of other artwork were found. The everyday tools of the bakers and fullers (clothmakers) and taverna owners (take-out food stands) all were on view for the first time in two thousand years. This city would provide historians with enough information to support years of reinterpretation.

The walls of the homes that were excavated at Pompeii were covered with elaborate frescoes and painted plaster. The walls shown here were found in the House of Vetti.

This is one of Pompeii's thermopolia, an ancient snack shop. Hot food that was sold to customers was kept in the round containers sunken into the counter. Some thermopolia had decorated rooms that might have been used as fancier dining areas.

Herculaneum was a much smaller town than Pompeii, but it provided even greater finds. Here the pyroclastic flow had not collapsed the walls of buildings. Everything was frozen in place. The food still sits on the tables abandoned by the fleeing citizens. The wooden doors and window frames have been carbonized in place by the heat of the flow. The grain still stands in the storage bins. In the baths the large basin that was thrown from its pedestal leans against the wall across the room.

Historians were delighted by the breadth and scope of all of the artifacts they were finding. But there was also a great mystery here—there was very little evidence that people had perished in Herculaneum as a result of this disaster. Historians studying the site concluded that the inhabitants of Herculaneum had been able to escape in time, unlike those of Pompeii. With that conclusion, their excavations were complete (only a small part of Herculaneum can be excavated since the rest of it lies under the modern town of Ercolano); and the site was opened to the public.

This view of the Herculaneum archaeological area shows how well preserved the town was. The walls of the houses still stand, including some that are several stories high.

Then a grisly discovery was made. Archaeologists had previously found three skeletons in what would have been the beach area of Herculaneum at the time of the eruption of Mount Vesuvius. These skeletons were thought to represent the few people who had not arrived at the beach in time to escape by water. But in 1982 archaeologists excavated some storage areas along the beach site. What they found was shocking: "The chambers . . . were filled with the skeletons of people who obviously had met sudden death . . . a household in flight: seven adults, four children, and a baby lying cradled . . . [in] the next [chamber] . . . a host of tangled, charred skeletons including that of a horse . . . a Roman soldier." There were the remains of a woman wearing expensive gold jewelry; another woman, pregnant, dead with the bones of the unborn child still inside her. Sadly, there was a boat and a man holding an oar. Why did this boat not leave with some of the people found here on it?

In 1982, an archaeologist excavates the buried skeleton of one of the inhabitants that couldn't escape Herculaneum.

Since the Romans cremated their dead, these bodies gave historians their first look at actual Romans. Here was a chance to learn more about their lives—their nutrition, clothing, stature, almost everything about the way they would have looked at the time of the eruption. It also forced historians to revise their entire story of what happened in Herculaneum on August 24, A.D. 79. Gone was the idea that only the city was buried, unlike at Pompeii. One can only imagine the last moments of these frightened people of Herculaneum huddled in the storage caves by the sea, hoping to be rescued.

Herculaneum and Pompeii provide many artifacts for historians to use to piece together the story of the people who lived and died here. As historian Salvatore Nappo notes: "What the excavations in the Vesuvius area produced was an intact image of ancient life, almost as if in suspended animation, undamaged by the passing of the centuries." Each new piece of the puzzle that is found forces historians to reinterpret and rewrite the story of this remarkable event that, two thousand years later, gives us a window onto one tragic day in the life of the Roman Empire.

## CHAPTER 13

# When Poetry Is History—
# The Search for Homer's Troy

In 1987 a 102-year-old African American woman became a sensation in Vermont. A videotape recording showed her reciting the history of generations of her family from their years as slaves through the events of her own life in Vermont. Everyone was amazed at her recall of details of events that occurred long before her time. What people saw is a skill that was essential in all societies before history was written down—oral history. At one time, oral history was the only way to hand down memories of the past to future generations. Children were specially trained to repeat stories, often in verse form, until they had them accurately memorized. Adult "storytellers" would be responsible for passing on the stories to the next generation. In this way, history was transmitted from generation to generation without written records. It was, naturally, not a perfect method of record keeping. The wisdom of the group could be lost if the adult storyteller died before training a young replacement. In spite of the care taken to be accurate, discrepancies were also bound to creep in over the generations. However, even with these drawbacks, many of the oral histories that were eventually written down have proved to be quite accurate in their details.

Modern societies tend to mistrust the oral tradition, assuming that it would be impossible for anyone to memorize enough information to ensure the survival of the history of a society. It is also assumed that oral history deteriorates over time, until it can no longer be viewed as anything more than legend. A very famous example of oral history was viewed in this way until a determined amateur archaeologist proved the legend to be factual.

Homer was a blind Greek poet who lived in the ninth or eighth century B.C. His most famous works, the *Iliad* and the *Odyssey*, recount a series of stories from the time of the Trojan War. Until 1870, the accepted historical consensus was that Homer's Troy was a work of fiction, a story that was part of Greek mythology and meant to be enjoyed as a "hero" adventure tale.

Most scholars believed that Troy had never existed. One historian comments about amateur archaeologist Heinrich Schliemann's search for Troy, "When Schliemann began excavating at Hissarlik in 1870, probably about half of the scholars . . . would have said that Homer's Troy was a figment of his imagination and that to seek its location . . . was folly."

Serious archaeologists of the time had not even attempted to find the location of Troy or any of the Homeric sites. Homer lived long after a Trojan War would have occurred, if, in fact, such a conflict ever took place. He would have had no way of obtaining firsthand information from survivors. His accounts were filled with "casual, scattered bits of information . . . such as any poet might freely imagine about any royal stronghold, king and people." There was simply no reason to assume that there was any semblance of reality behind these wonderful sagas.

Historians had not allowed for the major role that oral history played in the society in which Homer lived. He might indeed have lacked firsthand knowledge of the war. However, he had access to something almost as valuable, "a core of very old stories, recited and reshaped by bards over centuries." The Greeks at the time of Homer were only then becoming a literate people who kept a written record. Homer had access to actual accounts; this is indicated in some of the "Bronze Age details that no one in Homer's Iron Age would have known," according to one researcher of this period.

Heinrich Schliemann could not have known of the modern records that now seem to point to a strong oral history that Homer could have used. Schliemann simply was enthralled with the stories of the Trojan War, and he was determined to find Troy and the other cities named in the epics. He rejected the common historical thinking that Troy, if it existed, would have to be at Bounarbashi. His reading of Homer led him to select a large hill called Hissarlik, located about 4 miles (6 km) from the Dardenelles in Turkey, the waterway that connects the Black Sea to

German archaeologist Heinrich Schliemann was convinced that Homer's Troy really existed, and he was determined to find it. Schliemann is yet another archaeologist who ultimately rewrote history.

the Mediterranean Sea, which some historians believed was the least promising choice. Schliemann arrived "with only pickaxes, wooden shovels, baskets, and eight wheelbarrows." Over several years he dug trenches and uncovered a series of cities that had been built on the site. He believed that he had found Troy in the lowest of these cities. Later archaeologists and historians would believe that he had actually dug through the historical Troy (sixth of the nine cities on the site), and that the site he claimed was Troy actually predated the city of the Trojan War.

The city walls, houses, and stashes of gold and silver that he found were important; but not as important as the fact that he had proved a mythical city to be real. Several years later, he also located and excavated another of the cities of the Homeric epics, Mycenae. Schliemann could not resist chiding those who still

The "treasure of Priam" is a hoard of metal and semi-precious stones that were found at the Hissarlik site excavated by Heinrich Schliemann between 1871 and 1890.

doubted him: "It would seem that my critics were in the wrong and not myself," he wrote in 1881.

Critics he did have in plenty. When Schliemann announced his discovery of Troy, he caused an uproar among traditional historians. One researcher notes that Schliemann's announcement of his find was followed by "a crop of books and pamphlets . . . for there were many professional scholars . . . who considered themselves better qualified to judge on Homer than he." As controversial as his findings were, over time he convinced historians that Homer had been presenting history, not just a fictional epic, in the *Iliad* and the *Odyssey*.

"It can no longer be doubted . . . that there really was an actual historical Trojan War in which a coalition of Achaeans, or Mycenaeans, . . . fought against the people of Troy and their allies," says a modern researcher. Homer told a story based on the oral histories he heard. The story lived on over all the years because it was also a wonderful epic that enthralled its readers. However, it took the determination and imagination of Heinrich Schliemann to find the pieces of the puzzle that gave Homer the credit for being a historian first and a storyteller second. From the artifacts of Troy and Mycenae came the proof that this great story was more than a myth, and that Homer had provided the pieces to help create a historical picture of the Trojan War.

Yet another puzzle remains for future researchers—many modern historians do not believe that Homer was an actual person and think that his epics represent a set of oral stories written down after the time when he would have lived. Others believe that Homer represents two poets who composed the stories at about the same time and that over time, both poems were attributed to one person. We began this chapter with a "real" Homer and a mythical Troy. We end with a real Troy and a mythical Homer. It looks like this remains a puzzle in need of many more pieces!

## CHAPTER 14

# What Language Is This?— Understanding the Egyptians

**D**uring the summer of 2002, the National Gallery of Art, in Washington, D.C., presented an exhibit called "The Quest for Immortality: Treasure of Ancient Egypt." The exhibit displayed artifacts taken from Egyptian tombs—funerary masks, canopic jars, jewelry, a sarcophagus (coffin), and even a historically accurate reconstruction of an Egyptian burial chamber. Long lines of visitors waited patiently to view these items.

The organizers of the exhibit knew that the ancient Egyptians and their burial customs continue to intrigue people today. The Egyptians, who spent much of their resources in a quest for immortality, have certainly gained immortal fame. For centuries people have visited their great pyramids and lined up for any chance to see a mummy and any other ancient Egyptian artifacts up close.

This fascination with Egyptian items probably came about because for many years, they could only be admired, not understood. The puzzle they represented intrigued all who saw them. Historians questioned how the pyramids were built, why certain items were included with burials, and how bodies were mummified to preserve them. But the most fascinating mystery over the years was the hieroglyphics (picture writing) left by the pyramid builders. As one historian noted, "Every monument was covered in inscriptions, and nobody could read a word of them." These people built for the future and left behind a detailed record of their accomplishments so that their story would never be forgotten. Unfortunately, after all their efforts, their message could not be understood.

However, they had left behind a key to what they had written, a key not found for thousands of years. Displayed at the British Museum in London is a black stone covered with inscrip-

Ancient Egyptian monuments are covered with hieroglyphics like this that historians were unable to decipher.

tions. It is not particularly large—only about 3.5 feet by 2 feet (1 by 0.5 meter). But it is one of the most important artifacts ever found.

The stone was found near the town of Rosetta, in Egypt, by one of the Emperor Napoleon's soldiers in 1799. Clearly the writing on the stone is in three different alphabets. Very quickly, it became an object of intense interest to linguists and historians. They worked until 1822, when the stone's inscriptions were fully deciphered. What was discovered was that the same message was written three times on the stone—first in ancient Egyptian, next in a later form of Egyptian known as demotic (or commonly used), and at the bottom in Greek. Although many historians worked to decipher the stone, credit is usually given to Jean François Champollion, who was the first to decipher the entire message and publish it for the world.

With his translation, the messages left on the walls of the tombs and on the grave goods could finally be deciphered. In the words of one historian: "Suddenly . . . the span of recorded history expanded by some two millennia; the pharaohs began to

By deciphering the three languages on the Rosetta Stone, historians could finally read the Egyptians' hiero-glyphics and learn a great deal about their lives.

speak to us directly through their stone monuments, wall paintings and papyrus manuscripts." Many of the puzzles associated with Egyptian antiquities could be solved based on this knowledge. Now historians could return to the tombs and read the accounts that the hieroglyphs told of the lives of the pharaohs. They could read the inscriptions on the grave goods that told of their intended use. From this time on, any discovery could be "read" and understood.

In 1922 one of the greatest discoveries of Egyptian relics ever made took place when archaeologist Howard Carter opened the tomb of the Pharoah Tutankhamen. Notes one historian: "No archaeological discovery has ever captured the public imagination in the same way, or to the same extent." The tomb was plain on the outside; perhaps this protected it from the damage done to other tombs by treasure seekers over the centuries. Within the tomb, Carter found the most impressive collection of funerary goods from the ancient world ever seen, from a funeral mask of "solid gold inlaid with semi-precious stones and glass-paste," to all the grave goods buried with the pharaoh for use in his next life—chariots, candlesticks, ritual clothing, jewelry, statues, models of boats, cups, and food items.

Carter carefully documented every item he found, giving historians the opportunity to study such a tomb as a complete unit. Historians happily immersed themselves in studying the items found in the "richest burial ever to have been found in the Valley of the Kings." But without the knowledge gained from the Rosetta Stone one hundred years earlier, this would have been just another puzzling pile of beautiful gold grave goods. Its meaning was discovered through that black stone.

From that one artifact, all others found before or since that had written text were given meaning. It is extremely rare that any one artifact could serve as such a powerful new way to interpret the past. Even more rare is the puzzle that can be solved with just one piece. The Rosetta Stone is such a puzzle—the piece that allowed the "long inscriptions, beautiful as sculpture,

**Understanding the Etruscan alphabet of Rongorongo would give historians much knowledge about the Etruscan peoples whose culture disappeared when Rome became an empire.**

explaining who made them and when and why" to finally fit, and the message from the Egyptians' ancient past to be read in the modern world.

Historians and linguists (language experts) are still working to decipher other untranslated languages today. Linguists hope to understand the statues of Easter Island by deciphering Rongorongo. Other linguists work with the Zapotec language of Mexico, the Indus from Pakistan and India, and the Meroitic of the Sudan. Who knows what pieces of the historical puzzle might be found if these lost languages could be understood.

CHAPTER 15

# Is the Bible History?—
# The Story of Noah's Ark

Historians and archaeologists of early history know that they are working with limited sources of information—few primary sources and scarce artifacts and historic sites that are difficult to interpret. Not only were few people able to leave a written record, but many of those written records were lost over time. As a result, historians of early humankind tend to acknowledge openly that their interpretations are just theories. They put forth those theories with meticulous research and great vigor. However, most acknowledge that there is room for discussion and disagreement about their interpretations. Their objectivity makes the study of early history more an intellectual than an emotional exercise.

One major exception to this theoretical and dispassionate study and interpretation of ancient history occurs when historians try to determine the historical basis and validity of Old Testament accounts in the Bible. The Old Testament is the basic historical document for three of the world's major religions—Judaism, Christianity, and Islam. When an attempt is made to determine what is called the "historicity" of the Bible (whether the events mentioned in it are historically true), the theoretical gets mixed up with real emotions that come from belief or disbelief in basic religious tenets. Other cultural groups encounter similar controversies over beliefs, but the furor over the historicity of the Bible is certainly the most vocal.

Old Testament stories have been the subjects of numerous research papers, books, and television programs. Researchers in this area not only tend to lose any objectivity, but fight fiercely. They disagree about the story of creation and how the Old Testament account fits with the known geological age of the earth; or about the location of the Garden of Eden; or about the location of the mountain where Moses received the Ten Commandments. Historians face the problem that the Bible is seen by many believers as exact, dated, historical truth. It is seen by others as a "faith story," which tells of God's covenant, or pact, with his people. In this view, although the Bible speaks of historical people, it makes no attempt to be "accurate" in the way that we expect accuracy in historical accounts of today. These problems are well illustrated by the search to find out whether the story of Noah's Ark is historically true. If the flood story is true, historians want to determine precisely when and where it occurred.

Most of the existing documentary records for the earliest civilizations are agricultural trading records, usually written in local alphabets and numerical systems. Often these written records—and the oral traditions of other cultures—contain some reference to a massive flood, a deluge in which all are destroyed except for a small select group who then repopulate the earth. The flood stories appear in wide ranging areas. The Miao or Miautso people of inland China have a flood story. So do the Australian aboriginal people and the Biami of Papua, New Guinea. The most famous account other than the one in the Bible is in the Epic of Gilgamesh, written in Mesopotamia sometime before 2000 B.C. For many historians, the sheer number of flood stories in both written and oral tradition confirms the validity of the biblical account.

Other researchers encountering this plethora of flood accounts see instead that the stories originate in societies based in areas prone to flooding. The biblical peoples lived primarily in the flood plains of the Tigris and Euphrates rivers, so they would be subject to periodic "great floods." For these researchers, the biblical story of a great flood is simply an exaggerated account of an actual historical flood.

Both sides tend to grow heated and passionate in defending their positions. While some historians point to geological studies of soil that show evidence of flooding, and even of great floods, other historians insist that this evidence proves that there was no single flood that covered the entire area at once.

Other debates concern the ark. The Bible speaks of its size in terms of "cubits," indicating the ark was 300 cubits long. Whole books have been written on what this measurement actually represents in terms of our system of measures today. Websites offer estimates of the length of the ark that vary from 360 feet to 3,000 feet (108 to 900 meters). The number most commonly seen is 450 feet (135 meters).

The measurement problem points to an additional complication in interpreting the historicity of the Bible—the translation problem, which concerns alphabet and number systems. The date of the great flood is disputed because there is no agreement about interpreting the dating systems in the existing records. Historian Robert M. Best proposes a theory that Noah was Ziusudra, king of Shuruppak, an ancient Sumerian city. Best notes that Ziusudra's life and the flood are documented in records that place him around 2900 B.C. These records use an early Sumerian alphabet and number system called SHE-GUR. They would later have been translated into the new cuneiform alphabet used during the "Old Babylonian" period (1800–1600 B.C.). Best notes that "a different scribe, perhaps a student scribe,

Artists throughout the ages have presented the different interpretations of the Noah's Ark story in their art. Notice the size and construction of the boats in these two paintings, one of which was done in the nineteenth century (above) and the other in the fifteenth century.

translated these numbers into cuneiform" and accidentally assumed that the original records used a different numbering system. A thousand years later, the person translating the records into Hebrew would not know that they had already been mistranslated and thus would not have corrected the text. If Best is correct, Ziusudra and the flood in Shuruppak would correspond exactly to the biblical Noah. It is easy to see how language confusion, added to the conflicting stories of the flood in old accounts, could make any attempt to historically place and date these events almost impossible.

Other lengthy studies dispute such issues as the translation of the word "mountain." There is an ongoing dispute over whether "mountain" was used in the same sense that we use it today; perhaps the term should be translated as "hill," since the people living in this area in ancient times had no knowledge of high mountains. That, in turn, could radically change the interpretations of the biblical account that the ark came to rest on Mount Ararat, in present-day Turkey. Since many millions of dollars have been spent by researchers attempting to locate the remains of the ark on Mount Ararat, this theory generates much controversy.

There is a great deal of historical data to work with, so the problem here is not the usual lack of puzzle pieces for interpretation. We actually have more written information available about these events than one would expect for this time period. Problems arise because of the beliefs that the investigators bring to the information—the clash between religious faith and science.

In September 2000, the famous undersea explorer Robert Ballard announced that remains of a human civilization had been located under the Black Sea off the coast of Turkey. The ruins included a building "characteristic of stone-age structures built seven thousand years ago in the interior of Turkey," Ballard said in an interview with CNN. Also found were "carved wooden beams, wooden branches, and stone tools." There was immediate speculation in the media that what had been found was evidence of the flood in the Noah's Ark story. The response from those who believe that the Bible is a literal account was swift. The website called "Answers in Genesis" responded that Ballard was trying "to undermine the integrity of the biblical account . . . tantamount to declaring that God is a liar."

The issue here is not who is correct. Perhaps this is a historical puzzle that cannot be solved. Rather the issue is that such strong emotion, coupled with the more usual problems of interpreting old information, have made this one historical jigsaw that may never be assembled in such a way that the majority of historians, archaeologists, and researchers could agree on the picture it creates.

**CHAPTER 16**

# If Stones Could Speak—
# The Mysteries of the Stone Age

With this chapter we move into the time known as prehistory—the time for which there are no written records. At some of the historic sites of this period, we find a multitude of megaliths (literally, large stones)—stone structures up to six thousand years old. The stones may be arranged in a circle, called a henge; they may be arranged in rows, called an alignment. Others, covered over with flat stones, are thought to be passage tombs or wedge tombs. They are a great historical mystery and have given rise to intense speculation over the years.

Some theories to account for their existence have been quite unusual—including for example, that they were raised and placed into position by visitors from outer space. This is based on a belief that the technology needed to move the stones did not exist at the time in which the stones were raised.

Another fantastic theory is based on the fact that some of these stoneworks appear in Celtic countries. These theories attribute their construction to Druid magic. A popular variation on this theory is that Merlin, King Arthur's magician, arranged the stones for the most famous of these sites, Stonehenge, in Britain. In fact, Stonehenge was in place three thousand years before the legendary days of Merlin.

A series of these stone constructions in various countries are particularly noteworthy—those at Carnac in the Brittany region of France, at Avebury not far from Stonehenge, and at Newgrange north of Dublin, Ireland. However, it is important to remember that there are countless other examples of these primarily stone circles that are smaller, but that date from the same time period. These sites were not a rare occurrence, but rather a common part of the everyday lives of the Neolithic (Stone Age) people.

Some of the stone structures seem to have been designed to serve as giant calendars that marked important times of the year for an agricultural community. A Stonehenge guidebook notes that "the axis of the Sarcen [a type of stone] stone circle points

Carnac, France, is home to one of the world's greatest prehistoric monuments—a collection of nearly three thousand standing stones.

roughly to where an observer at the centre of Stonehenge would see the sunrise on the longest day of the year, in its most northerly position on the horizon," while other observers believe that what are known as "Station Stones" mark "settings of the sun and the moon."

In Ireland, a stone structure in the Boyne Valley north of Dublin, called Newgrange, is thought to date from 3200 B.C. It "is one of the finest examples . . . in Western Europe, of the type of tomb known as a passage-grave." At first regarded as a grave site, it was discovered that "on the winter solstice (shortest day of the year in December), rays of sun enter the tomb and light up the burial chamber, making it the oldest solar observatory in the world."

Others theorize that these sites are "temples," religious sites used by the Neolithic peoples. The Avebury stone circle in Britain is much larger and older than neighboring Stonehenge. It is seen as "strongly connected with the great human themes of fertility, life and death" because of "evidence of funerary feasts"

The passage-grave at Newgrange is the most famous of all Irish prehistoric monuments.

and the "deliberately paired together" stones that symbolize the "close connection between fertility and funerary rites."

Some of the smaller and less famous sites can provide an interesting look at the daily life of Neolithic peoples. What is striking about the Drombeg Stone Circle, not far from Skibbereen, Ireland, is not so much the circle of seventeen stones that mark the winter solstice, but the cooking circle off to the side of the henge. A sign at the site states that experiments to test the effectiveness of Stone Age cooking methods were carried out here. Historians know that meat was cooked by boiling it in a carefully defined area within circles such as this. Heated stones would be placed into the cold water to bring it to boiling. An experiment showed that the same quantity of water would be brought to cooking temperatures faster using this method than on a modern stove. Experiments like these are called reconstruction archaeology or experimental archaeology. Historians attempt to learn by reconstructing activities in hopes that there will be something in the process that is enlightening.

A number of years ago a group of engineers and historians joined to refute some of the more far-fetched theories about the creation of the stone circles. They attempted to duplicate the raising of the large stones at Stonehenge. Using the tools of the time and experimenting with different methods of transport and construction, they were able to quarry large stones, move them uphill to a site, dress them (shape them with stone tools), and raise them into position. "With a deft use of sledges, rails, ropes, ramps, pivot blocks, and 'tilting stones,' as few as 100 people would have been needed to move and raise the 40-ton Stonehenge uprights." In this way, historians established that outside intervention—or magic—would not have been needed to create these stone observatories. Similar experiments have been done at pyramids and at other early sites involving sophisticated engineering.

Experiments such as these cannot tell us today exactly how these people lived, but they can help formulate theories that account for the artifacts that the Neolithic people left behind. This is not historical evidence itself, of course, but it at least allows historians to give these people the credit they deserve for their notable achievements. Perhaps it also gives historians the chance to observe that these older civilizations possessed skills of their own that, while not as technologically advanced as ours, still show them to be as intelligent and inventive as modern peoples. Sometimes, it seems that historians must fabricate their own puzzle pieces to make their interpretation of the past as accurate as possible.

## CHAPTER 17

# When the Only Message Is Cave Drawings

In the time period ten to twenty-five thousand years earlier than the Stone Age, we find artifacts that are easier to interpret than those of the Neolithic period. At several places around the world, caves filled with wonderful engravings and/or paintings have been discovered.

These early cave drawings were created by early humans from about fifteen to thirty thousand years ago. The most famous of these caves are in Southern France. Among them, the caves at Lascaux contain paintings that, in the words of one art historian, provide "our earliest tangible trace, our first sign of art and also of man . . . 'Lascaux Man' created . . . this world of art in which communication between individual minds begins." Earlier paintings may exist, but these are currently considered to be the best preserved and most complete ever found.

These early humans left us a pictorial record of their lives. These are artifacts in themselves. However, in a real sense, these are also primary sources—a record "written," or, in this case, drawn, that preserves a history. From this record we can "read" what was important in their lives by noting their choices of subjects to paint or scratch into the stone.

The caves at Lascaux were discovered in 1940 by four boys who were investigating a hole in the ground where a tree had been uprooted a number of years before. Prehistorians who had always defined man by his tool-making abilities had a momentous discovery to deal with. Until then, prehistorians believed that Stone Age, or Neolithic, man used stone tools, Iron Age man used the first metal tools, and so on. Tool-making is found early in prehistory, in a time where humans are still not considered to have fully evolved into *Homo sapiens,* the man who thinks. Prehumans were already using tools, but art was something that moved beyond tool-making, as art historian Georges Bataille notes: "Art begins with full-grown man . . . the shift from the world of work to the world of play." But prehistorians never expected to find such ancient or wonderful examples of this art.

The art of Lascaux is the art of the cave dweller's everyday life—the animals that he saw, hunted, and imagined. There are horses and cows, bulls more than 15 feet (4.5 meters) long, deer and bison, rhinoceros, ibex, and even a unicorn. The colors are bold, bright reds, yellows, and browns. Only rarely does the cave art depict human figures.

This poses yet another mystery for historians. The animals are beautifully drawn and easily recognizable. The few human figures, on the other hand, are stick figures, often half-animal and half-human. Why would these great artists who could obviously draw so wonderfully from nature, draw a human figure so poorly? Those who study the work think that perhaps there was some sort of cultural taboo against drawing humans. It is a mystery that is not likely to be solved, but one that provides historians with ample opportunities for re-analysis and reinterpretation.

A rock painting of bison in the caves of Lascaux

Another mystery is that at all the caves, the artists tend to reuse the same surface. At Combarelles, where the interior is covered with engravings, the tour guide can stand at one point and trace with his flashlight three or four animals obviously superimposed one on top of another. Notes one historian: "the cave has . . . successive re-paintings . . . all visible through each other. This is a constant phenomenon in pre-historic art." With all of the caves available, why reuse the surface in one cave rather than just move on to another surface?

Theories hold that perhaps only certain caves were used, and that these might be "sacred" or ritual places. In this view, the paintings and engravings are religious in nature, a sort of "prayer" for a good hunt in which the hunters will find the animals they have pictured here. Again, this is a mystery for which there is no real solution. Bataille notes in conclusion that, "It is not probable that the painted, or engraved, images were simply meant as a durable kind of decoration."

Another mystery is that the artists created their work under difficult conditions. The tourist at Combarelles today crouches over, following the guide along a narrow, winding path. Halfway through the tour the guide points out a line of sediment running horizontally under the engraved walls at about waist level. That line marks the original floor of the cave, which has been dug out to allow access for visitors. The original artwork was done by people who crawled into caves less than 3 feet (1 meter) high, sometimes significantly less. With only a primitive torch for light, the artist spent hours cutting his design onto the wall.

The difficulty of creating this artwork under these conditions gives rise to questions. What would motivate the artist to go through so much effort to get his or her work onto the wall? How did these people have the time to create this art? Did this arduous effort represent some form of religious ritual? In view of the confined space, were others even going to see the work so painstakingly carved onto the wall? Perhaps only the "priest" or "shaman" of the tribe had access or created the pictures. We can only speculate in attempting to resolve these questions.

Here in this early stage of prehistory we are given a tantalizing glimpse of the people from whom we descend. We learn just enough of their story to be intrigued by it and to want to know more. We also know that Lascaux and the other caves of this area of southwest France represent only a small fraction of the caves that were painted throughout the world around this time. New finds of painted caves are being announced frequently. Investigation of an aboriginal cave in Australia began in May 2003. The cave has "a series of 203 images in . . . eleven superimposed layers." This site was happened on by a hiker in 1995. The message left behind by the cave artists communicates much about their lives that we would not have known otherwise; however, the message provides nowhere near enough pieces to complete the picture.

CHAPTER 18

# Talking Skeletons—
# Lucy and the Development
# of Modern Man

What happens when history is so ancient that literally only small pieces survive? Long before recorded history, long before even the cave drawings, men and women roamed the earth. These ancestors of ours left us no record, written or pictorial, to help us tell their story. They did leave behind pieces of themselves—their bones.

We do not know how many of these ancestors there were. But we do know that only the smallest fraction of their remains has survived. From this evidence archaeologists, anthropologists, and historians try to re-create their lives. Each discovery of their bones was remarkable simply because so few were ever found. Each new discovery has also tended to force those who study them to rethink and revise the entire family tree of early man.

In 1974, one find revolutionized our thinking about early humans. Donald Johanson was the lucky anthropologist who discovered the most complete early skeleton ever found. He found "her" in Ethiopia and called her Lucy. It was later determined that Lucy was approximately 3.2 million years old. The oldest known tools were found with Lucy at the same site.

Lucy revealed a secret of early humans. They had begun to walk upright much earlier than anyone had realized. Upright walking is one of the differences that sets humans apart from apes, so this was important news. Lucy, more correctly known as *Australopithecus afarensis*, was only about 3 feet (1 meter) tall, even though she was an adult.

Before Lucy, the oldest and best skeleton studied dated from about seventy-five thousand years ago. As Johanson explained,

Paleoanthropologist Donald Johanson shows his discovery named Lucy, the skeleton of the most complete *Australopithecus afarensis* ever found.

"there *are* older hominid fossils, but they are all fragments." Lucy's significance lay in "her completeness and her great age." Because such a complete skeleton was found, anthropologists could significantly revise their knowledge of the development of humans.

Donald Johanson wrote about the "problem" his discovery caused for those who study hominids, or early man. At first, Johanson tried to fit his find into the existing paleoanthropological knowledge, but this set of bones—and the tools found with it—would not fit. It took years of study to determine Lucy's significance. In 1995, some scientists studying Lucy's bones decided "she" was a "he." Discussion continues, and the final answer may await another discovery. As Johanson says, "In paleoanthropology one does not have brilliant flashes of insight . . . recognition comes slowly."

Such studies of the earliest history of humans broke into the news again in 2002. *USA Today* carried a front-page story on the

French paleontologist Michel Brunet holds and discusses the Toumai skull with Doctor Mackaye Hassane Taisso (right) and Ahounta Djimdoumalbaye (left), the man who discovered the skull.

find of a skull, called Toumai, which means "hope of life," in a desert in Chad in Africa, in 2001. Professor Bernard Wood, an expert on hominids from George Washington University said: "It [Toumai skull] completely sidelines everything else that has been found that is older than a million and [a] half years."

The find is dated at six to seven million years old, making it the oldest skull ever found. It calls into question all current thinking about how humans evolved. As reporter Tim Friend notes in a related article, "Where different ancestors are placed on the tree is a matter of contentious debate among scientific camps." The *Washington Post* quoted a member of the team that discovered the skull, who noted that "it will never be possible to know precisely where or when [humans originated]." That is the critical point.

This find is a fitting case study in the exploration of how we assemble history. From modern-day mysteries back to our oldest origins, the process is actually the same. History is about attempting to complete a complex puzzle with pieces of information that come in many different forms, ranging from old bones to written narratives. History seeks to create the most complete and accurate story about our past.

## CHAPTER 19

# Who Owns History?
# Zeugma, Chancellorsville,
# the World Trade Center

O n opposite banks of the Euphrates River in Turkey lie
the remains of two ancient Roman cities, connected
by a bridge. Together they were called Zeugma, which
translates roughly as "bridge" or "junction." In some ways
Zeugma is no different from countless other old Roman sites forgotten by time. Buried beneath the ground are the remains of
villas with wonderful wall frescoes and floor mosaics. No doubt
the remains of Roman baths, temples, amphitheaters, theaters,
and fora are also buried there. But Zeugma is different from
other Roman ruins because it has disappeared under the waters
of a reservoir that feeds a new hydroelectric dam.

   One of the most difficult and troubling facts of life in historical research today is that many promising historic sites lie in the
path of modern development. When such sites are discovered,

fierce arguments take place between developers and historians and archaeologists. Who owns history?

When it was announced that the dam under construction on the Euphrates would destroy the site of Zeugma, two things happened. First, looters, knowing that the site would soon disappear, began digging to find "treasures" that might be hidden at the site. Next, archaeologists, recognizing that the site would soon be lost to them forever, proposed to undertake a "salvage archaeology," in which attempts are made to remove as much information as fast as possible. One archaeologist notes that "At Zeugma pottery and tile fragments were thickly strewn across the surface; coins, glass, tesserae [pieces of mosaics], gemstones . . . were frequently brought up in plowing . . . traces of large buildings were evident . . . [This] pointed to a large and complex urban site with a wide range of structures."

A PBS television program documented the final dig done at Zeugma just before the site was flooded. A bulldozer is rarely seen on any archaeological dig because bulldozers frequently destroy portions of the site they are attempting to uncover. However, researchers using a bulldozer discovered a fourteen-room villa filled with exceptional mosaic tile floors. With only two weeks remaining before the flooding would begin, researchers scrambled to document the site and remove the mosaics to a museum. Historians studied the information found in the hastily excavated layers. They wanted to answer a long-standing question about damage done to the city in an invasion in A.D. 250. The soon-to-be-buried evidence was their last chance to solve this part of the historical puzzle. Based on an analysis of the material found in soil layers, they determined that a catastrophic fire, which caused the site to be abandoned, had occurred. This happened at a time that corresponds to a Persian invasion of the area.

Dr. Gaetano Palumbo, Director of Archaeological Conservation for the World Monuments Fund, is deeply concerned by situations like Zeugma: "Salvage work does not allow for adequate

This is the excavation of Zeugma before the city was flooded in order to build a dam.

scientific work, so in the end it becomes a kind of treasure hunt in which we just try to retrieve things. That's a pity." He acknowledges that sometimes salvage work is all that time will allow, and that archaeologists must "make the best of the situation." The same kind of salvage archaeology took place in China from 1992 to 2003, until the Three Gorges Dam on the Yangtze River became operational, flooding about 1,200 sites considered to be historically important.

Who owns history? How do we strike a balance between the need to preserve the past and the needs of modern life? These questions are receiving increased attention in both scholarly journals and the media. In the United States, historic sites are often much younger than many of those around the world. Even so, the same issues arise. An organization called the Civil War Preservation Trust (CWPT), for example, continuously monitors development near Civil War battlefield sites. This organization has participated in many legal attempts to stop development, particularly those encroaching on important sites in Virginia. Fierce opposition faces developers seeking to build houses near the battlefield at Chancellorsville, near Fredericksburg, Virginia, for example. Their proposed use of land associated with the crucial Battle of Chancellorsville, and the possibility of spoiling viewing corridors that help people understand military action at the site are contested. Preservation proponent Jim Campi states: "The fate of Chancellorsville battlefield hangs in the balance. . . . Plans for a megalopolis on the 790-acre [316-hectare] Mullins Farm are moving forward. If built, this city will . . . destroy the Chancellorsville experience forever."

Many argue that such a demand for preservation does not allow for the need for conveniently located housing or shopping, and that enough important sites have already been designated by the National Park Service as protected battlefields. The Civil War Preservation Trust argues that much of the land not currently protected is needed for use in understanding past events that played an important role in history. Once lost, they say, this land can never be retrieved. An archaeologist writes in CWPT's quarterly newsletter, *Hallowed Ground,* "Battlefields are special places. They, and only they, can provide the answers to many of the questions . . . once lost, they can never be replaced, rebuilt or restored."

All of us must understand that the need to preserve the past is not a simple issue. A "fair" solution can be difficult to formulate in most cases. How does a society value the claims made by those whose civilization was destroyed in the period of European conquest and colonization? For example, are Native American claims for compensation for the loss of their vast territories to be resolved by returning the land to them? What happens then to the hundreds of millions of people who live on it today? How does society balance the fact that terrible errors were made in dealing with native or aboriginal peoples throughout the world with the needs of large modern populations who now occupy those peoples'

In 2003, building construction in Manhattan, New York, uncovered the remains of more than four hundred former African slaves. A horse-drawn funeral hearse followed by hundreds of people carried the coffins to be reburied after the African Burial Ground Memorial Project ceremony.

lands? Is it enough that token sites be preserved—sacred burial sites of African Americans or native peoples—and that the errors of the past be acknowledged? Increasingly, today's citizens are being asked to look back on the activities of their ancestors and find a way to correct errors of the past.

We must also consider the issue of who owns items removed from conquered countries by colonial powers. In July 2003, the Egyptian government demanded that the British Museum return the Rosetta Stone. There have been demands for art and items such as the Elgin Marbles—the marble frieze from the Parthenon in Athens, Greece—to be returned to the countries that originally produced and owned them. This controversial issue is at the base of heated discussions about ownership and fairness. Major museums, including the British Museum in London, the Berlin Museum, the Metropolitan Museum of Art in

New York, the State Hermitage Museum in Saint Petersburg, and the Vatican Museums in Rome hold items whose possession is contested by their original owners.

Who owns history? This question properly recognizes that all of us are part of the process of making history. For example, at Zeugma and Civil War battlefield sites, the question also acknowledges the importance of maintaining intact those historic places so that we can continue to learn about the past or pay tribute to its relevance and importance.

Relevance and importance figure prominently in the discussion about what to do with the site of the Twin Towers of the World Trade Center, in New York City. The terrorist attack of

The importance of the site where the Twin Towers of the World Trade Center used to be was demonstrated when the New York City mayor, as well as the architects and developer, unveiled the design for Freedom Tower in 2005. This design would make it the strongest and safest building in the world.

September 11, 2001, brought destruction of the buildings and great loss of lives. In the debate over what should be erected on that site, the words most often heard about the location say that it is "sacred ground." This calls to mind President Abraham Lincoln's account of the Civil War battlefield at Gettysburg: ". . . the brave men, living and dead, who struggled here, have consecrated it, far above our poor power to add or detract. The world . . . can never forget what they did here."

Many believe that ground hallowed by significant historic events and grievous loss of life must be held apart from other uses. It must memorialize and honor those who experienced the events in some way, such as marking the federal office building site of the Oklahoma City bombing on April 19, 1995; the Texas School Book Depository building, where John F. Kennedy's assassin lay in wait for him on November 22, 1963; and other sites where momentous events took place. The need to mark the spot, to memorialize the event so that it will not be forgotten in the future, shows the power of history in our lives. We want to ensure that no elements of the historical events in our lives will be lost or forgotten.

## EPILOGUE

# Can We Ever Be Sure?

What all the stories in this book have in common is the difficulty of finding a completely factual picture of the event. Whether for modern events with a great deal of information available or for historical places and events with very little documentation, there never seems to be enough information to reconstruct the entire picture. And sometimes the pieces of information contradict each other. An event as well-documented as the sinking of the *Edmund Fitzgerald* leaves historical questions unanswered. If we could create a time machine and visit the event as it was happening, we might still be unable to tell exactly what took place.

Even if we cannot be as accurate as we would like, the stories show us that more information leads to a better picture. Thus, what is important is acquiring more information about the past. One development that will aid historians in this search is ever more sophisticated technology. Documentation about the present is significantly better now than it was even a few years ago. Information technology such as the Internet and the World Wide Web make it possible to save many viewpoints of an event. Future historians interpreting our times will have access to more pieces of the puzzle than we have had.

The story of the Lake Champlain gunboats shows how technology has changed underwater archaeology over the last century. New technologies just coming into use may revolutionize land-based archaeology as well. Most archaeological sites today are only partially excavated—sometimes only one tenth of the site is dug. Archaeologists do this deliberately to preserve the site for future digs when technology may provide more information with less impact on the integrity of the site. Other sites such as the terra-cotta warriors of the tomb of the first emperor of China are being partially reburied to protect them from further deterioration until better techniques are found to preserve them. Some even expect that future archaeologists will not have to dig to determine what lies buried. Imaging technology is expected to become much more sophisticated, so machines may give historians a perfect picture of buried artifacts without disturbing the terrain.

Another common theme of stories in this book is how unexpected many of the historical discoveries are. Often, even when locations and events are known, details become more and more obscure over time. Thus, the Colonial Williamsburg archaeologists actually hoped to find nothing and instead located one of the earliest American settlements. People unexpectedly found ruins at Pompeii and Herculaneum, even though a base of knowledge existed as to where they should be found. We need to be alert to the possibility that history is hidden all around us.

It is also evident how often lack of understanding the language or the historical context of the event hampers the search for the right puzzle pieces. Even when the Egyptians tried to record their history for the future, over time translation became a problem. The language of an ancient civilization may totally disappear, as was the case with the Egyptians. Records can be translated incorrectly, as may have happened in the story of Noah and his ark. A people's language may take the form of pictures, as in the Lascaux cave drawings, whose meaning to the cave dwellers we can only guess at. We cannot expect to correctly understand historical events if we cannot understand the people of the past. In many historical investigations, the message is not getting through. We need to keep looking for the best way to figure out what the people of the past tell us in the records they left behind.

Fact and myth have often become intertwined; from our distant vantage point, they become difficult to separate. To a degree we can sort out some of these myths over time through additional research. For example, Homer's "myth" about Troy was found to have a historical basis, and historians discovered that the Arthurian legends may relate to an actual historical person. Sometimes further research will prove that the event is indeed mythological rather than historical, as we saw with the Great Wall of China. Still other stories of history, such as the biblical story of Noah, have such a confusing historical basis that it cannot be verified. We have also seen how difficult it is to interpret history when emotion plays a role, whether the emotion results from questions involving religion, as in the Bible stories, or from national pride, as in the mythical Great Wall.

We have seen that sometimes just one piece is needed to make the puzzle clear. Understanding the Rosetta Stone opened up knowledge of an entire civilization that had been lost to us because we did not know its language. The finding of one skull can change all of the current theories on the early hominids simply because each piece is so rare that one find adds mightily to the body of knowledge. And we have seen historians trying to re-create the past in order to determine how our ancestors accomplished important tasks. They have experimented with ancient cooking techniques, attempted to build stone megaliths, or re-created Egyptian burial chambers—all attempts to make the picture of the past a little clearer.

Victors have written most of the records that describe what took place during critical conflicts between two competing civilizations, and this, too, can interfere with our understanding of the past. We saw the Aztecs and Inca peoples' role in history reduced to that of uneducated primitives by the Spanish. Today, historians often actively seek information about groups whose history has been ignored whether because they were conquered, or because they left no written record. Historians often attempt to become more inclusive in their view of what constitutes history, recognizing that we need to consider a wide range of participants' viewpoints in order to create the most accurate picture.

Finally, we have seen that it is necessary for us to be historical investigators because history may provide insights into challenges we face today. The site at Mesa Verde revealed a culture that may have fallen apart because it overused its natural resources. History may have some lessons that will allow us to avoid repeating the same mistakes.

These factors are the realities that historians, archaeologists, and all students of the past have to deal with when "making" history. These realities, however, also make history a wonderful search for information. There is always the feeling that somewhere out there may lie the answer to the historical puzzle that you are working to solve. Like a good detective story, history provides us with plenty of clues to keep us searching for the answer.

This concept of history as a living, changing body of knowledge is not the one taught in schools years ago. Living, changing history is an adventure—a quest for the answers to all the riddles of the past that have not been solved. Can we ever be sure that we have finally found *the* definitive solution to a particular historical riddle? Probably not. That is ultimately what makes history fun. It offers us all the opportunity to become the next Heinrich Schliemann, the amateur archaeologist, and find the missing piece that ties the puzzle together.

In March 2002, I stood at the end of an ancient Roman road in Italica in Spain. Within my view were all the mounds that represent a lost city. A half-mile away lay beautiful mosaics that had already been excavated. But most exciting were all the possibilities that lay buried beneath those mounds. Who knows what wonders remain to be found there—and on countless other sites throughout the world. All that history—all those wonderful pieces of the puzzle just waiting to be discovered!

# Source Notes

p. 6    Larry Sklenar, *To Hell with Honor: Custer and the Little Bighorn* (Norman: University of Oklahoma Press, 2000), p. xiii.

p.7     Douglas D. Scott, *They Died with Custer: Soldiers' Bones from the Battle of the Little Bighorn* (Norman: University of Oklahoma Press, 1998), p. 349.

p. 12   "The Great Fire of Rome," *Secrets of the Dead,* PBS broadcast, December 18, 2002. New York: WNET Educational Broadcasting Corporation, 2002.

p. 23   Joseph MacInnis, *Fitzgerald's Storm: The Wreck of the Edmund Fitzgerald* (Toronto: Macmillan Canada, 1997), p. 87.

p. 23   MacInnis, p. 87.

p. 23   Robert J. Hemming, *Gales of November: the Sinking of the Edmund Fitzgerald* (Chicago: Contemporary Books, 1981), p. 51.

p. 24   Hugh E. Bishop, *The Night the Fitz Went Down* (Duluth, MN: Lake Superior Port Cities, 2000), p. 4.

p. 24   Frederick Stonehouse, *The Wreck of the Edmund Fitzgerald* (Au Train, MI: The Studios, 1991), p. 68.

p. 24   Bishop, p. 138.

p. 26   Dan Vergano, "Deep-Sea Archaeology: A New Day Surfaces," *USA Today,* June 27, 2002, p. 10D.

p. 27   Glenn Oeland, "The H. L. Hunley: Secret Weapon of the Confederacy," *National Geographic,* July 2002, p. 82.

p. 28   Philip K. Lundeberg, *The Gunboat Philadelphia and the Defense of Lake Champlain in 1776* (Basin Harbor, VT: Lake Champlain Maritime Museum, 1995), p. 38.

p. 32   "Gunboat *Spitfire,*" Lake Champlain Maritime Museum Marine Research Institute website (www.lcmm.org/site/mri_arch_projects/gunboat_spitfire2.html).

p. 33   Susan Myra Kingsbury, *The Records of the Virginia Company of London* (Washington, D.C.: Government Printing Office, 1906–1935), vol. 3, p. 551.

p. 35   Ivor Noël Hume, *Martin's Hundred* (Charlottesville, VA: University Press of Virginia, 1979), p. 24.

p. 35   Hume, p. 148.

p. 37   Ivor Noël Hume, *Discoveries in Martin's Hundred* (Williamsburg, VA: The Colonial Williamsburg Foundation, 1983), pp. 23–24.

p. 38   "Is the Great Wall of China the only manmade object you can see from space?," *The Straight Dope* website (www.straightdope.com/classics/a2_092).

p. 39   Arthur Waldron, *The Great Wall of China: From History to Myth* (Cambridge: Cambridge University Press, 1990), p. 5.

p. 40  Leonard Everett Fisher, *The Great Wall of China* (New York: Macmillan, 1986), p. 15.

p. 40  Peter Hessler, "Chasing the Wall," *National Geographic,* January 2003, p. 8.

p. 40  Jonathan Fryer, *The Great Wall of China* (New York: A.S. Barnes and Company, 1975), pp. 13–14.

p. 41  Melinda Liu, "The Late Great Wall," *Newsweek*, July 29, 2002, p. 43.

p. 41  Waldron, pp. 27–28.

p. 42  George Clapp Vaillant, *Aztecs of Mexico* (Garden City, NY: Doubleday, Doran & Company, 1941), p. 1.

p. 43  Harvey C. Gardiner, *Naval Power in the Conquest of Mexico* (New York: Greenwood Press, 1956), pp. 44, 46.

p. 43  Vaillant, p. 13.

p. 44  Muriel Porter Weaver, *The Aztecs, Maya, and Their Predecessors* (New York: Harcourt Brace Jovanovich, 1981), p. 521.

p. 44  Robert M. Carmack et al., *The Legacy of Mesoamerica* (Upper Saddle River, NJ: Prentice Hall, 1996), p. 3.

p. 45  Peggy K. Liss, *Mexico Under Spain, 1521–1556* (Chicago: University of Chicago Press, 1975), pp. 42–43.

p. 45  Davíd Carrasco, *Moctezuma's Mexico: Visions of the Aztec World* (Niwot: University Press of Colorado, 1992), p. 96.

p. 47  Antonio Serrato-Combe, *The Aztec Templo Mayor: A Visualization* (Salt Lake City: The University of Utah Press, 2001), p. 7.

p. 47  Carrasco, p. 1.

p. 47  Michael A. Malpass, *Daily Life in the Inca Empire* (Westport, CT: Greenwood Press, 1996), p. xxvii.

p. 48  Vaillant, p. 13.

p. 49  Hans Li, *The Ancient Ones: Sacred Monuments of the Inka, Maya and Cliffdweller* (New York: City of Light Editions, 1994), p. 6.

p. 49  Li, p. 13.

p. 51  Duane A. Smith, *Mesa Verde National Park: Shadows of the Centuries* (Lawrence: University Press of Kansas, 1988), p. 5.

p. 52  Gilbert R. Wenger, *The Story of Mesa Verde National Park* (Mesa Verde National Park, CO: Mesa Verde Museum Association, 1980), p. 40.

p. 52  Smith, p. 5.

p. 52  J. Richard Ambler, *The Anasazi* (Flagstaff: The Museum of Northern Arizona, 1977), pp. 46–47.

p. 53  Gene S. Stuart, *America's Ancient Cities* (Washington, D.C.: National Geographic Society, 1988), p. 92.

p. 53  Jesse Walter Fewkes, *A Prehistoric Mesa Verde Pueblo and Its Peoples* (Washington, D.C., 1917), p. 463.

p. 53  Smith, p. 5.

p. 53  Robert H. Lister, *Mesa Verde National Park: Preserving the Past* (Mancos, CO: ARA Mesa Verde Company, 1987), p. 52.

p. 54  John Bartlett, *Familiar Quotations*, 16th edition (Boston: Little, Brown and Company, 1992), p. 588.

p. 56  William W. Fitzhugh, *Vikings: The North Atlantic Saga* (Washington, D.C.: Smithsonian Institution Press, 2000), p. 97.

p. 57  Priit J. Vesilind, "In Search of the Vikings," *National Geographic,* May 2000, p. 24.

p. 58  Helge Ingstad and Anne Stine Ingstad, *The Viking Discovery of America* (New York: Checkmark Books, 2001), p. 126.

p. 58  Ingstad, p. 126.

p. 60    Fitzhugh, p. 214.

p. 60    Vesilind, p. 27.

p. 61    Graham Ashton, *The Realm of King Arthur* (Newport, Isle of Wight: J. Arthur Dixon, 1974), p. 2.

p. 63    Leslie Alcock, *Arthur's Britain: History and Archaeology, AD 367–634* (New York: St. Martin's Press, 1971), p. 358.

p. 64    Alcock, p. 88.

p. 64    Geoffrey Ashe, *The Discovery of King Arthur* (Garden City, NY: Doubleday, 1985), p. 111.

p. 65    Ashe, p. 79.

p. 65    Ashe, p. 82.

p. 69    S. J. Keay, *Roman Spain* (Berkeley: University of California Press, 1988), p. 59.

p. 69    Francis Jowett Wiseman, *Roman Spain: An Introduction to the Roman Antiquities of Spain and Portugal* (London: Bell, 1956), p. 191.

p. 69    Keay, p. 134.

p. 70    Leonard A. Curchin, *Roman Spain: Conquest and Assimilation* (New York: Routledge, 1991), p. 105.

p. 71    Xavier Aquilué and others, *Tarraco: An Archaeological Guide* (Tarragona, Spain: Edicions El Mèdol, 1992), p. 46.

p. 71    "Italica: Colonia Aelia Augusta Italicensium" (Santiponce, Spain: Junta de Andalucia, Consejeria de Cultura.)

p. 73    George Howe, ed., *Roman Literature in Translation* (New York: Harper & Brothers, 1924), p. 613.

p. 73    Joseph Jay Deiss, *Herculaneum: Italy's Buried Treasure* (Malibu, CA: The J. Paul Getty Museum, 1989), p. 15.

p. 74    Ian Andrews, *Pompeii* (Cambridge: Cambridge University Press, 1978), p. 48.

p. 77    Rick Gore, "The Dead Do Tell Tales at Vesuvius," *National Geographic,* May 1984, p. 570.

p. 78    Salvatore Nappo, *Pompeii: A Guide to the Ancient City* (New York: Barnes & Noble Books, 1998), p. 6.

p. 80    David A. Trail, *Schliemann of Troy* (New York: St. Martin's Press, 1995), p. 301.

p. 80    Carl W. Blegen, *Troy and the Trojans* (New York: Frederick A. Praeger, 1963), p. 18.

p. 81    John Fleischman, "Homer's Bones," *Discover* magazine, July 2002, p. 61.

p. 81    Fleischman, p. 61.

p. 82    Heinrich Schliemann, *Ilios the city and country of the Trojans* (New York: Harper & Brothers, 1881), pp. 20–21.

p. 83    Schliemann, p. 20.

p. 83    J.M. Cook, *The Troad: An Archaeological and Topographical Study* (London: Oxford University Press, 1973), p. 15.

p. 83    Blegen, p. 20.

p. 85    Maeve Kennedy, *The History of Archaeology* (New York: Barnes & Noble Books, 2002), p. 58.

p. 87    Andrew Robinson, *Lost Languages: The Enigma of the World's Undeciphered Scripts* (New York: McGraw-Hill, 2002), p. 13.

p. 87    Christopher Frayling, *The Face of Tutankhamun* (London: Faber and Faber, 1992), p. xi.

p. 87    Christiane Desroches-Noblecourt, *Tutankhamen: Life and Death of a Pharaoh* (New York: New York Graphic Society, 1963), p. 115.

p. 87    Nicholas Reeves, *The Complete Tutankhamun* (New York: Thames and Hudson, 1990), p. 68.

p. 88  Kennedy, p. 58.

p. 91  Robert M. Best, *Noah's Ark and the Ziusudra Epic: Sumerian Origins of the Flood Myth* (Fort Myers, FL: Enlil Press, 1999), p. 31.

p. 93  Best, p. 113.

p. 93  "Undersea explorer finds new evidence of great flood." CNN.com, September 13, 2000.

p. 94  "Proof of Noah's Flood at the Black Sea?" Answers in Genesis website (www.answersingenesis.org/docs/4168.asp).

p. 97  *Stonehenge and Neighbouring Monuments* (London: English Heritage, 1995), p. 20.

p. 97  Claire O'Kelly, *Concise Guide to Newgrange* (Cork, Ireland: Houston Printers, 1996), p. 5.

p. 97  Lisa Gerard-Sharp and Tim Perry, *Ireland* (London: Dorling Kindersley, 1995), p. 238.

p. 98  Keith Sugden, *The Prehistoric Temples of Stonehenge & Avebury* (Andover, U.K.: Pitkin, 1994), pp. 28–30.

p. 98  David Roberts, "Romancing the Stones," *Smithsonian* magazine, July 2002, p. 88.

p. 100  Georges Bataille, *Lascaux, or, The Birth of Art* (Lausanne: Skira, 1955), p. 11.

p. 101  Bataille, p. 27.

p. 102  Fernand Windels, *The Lascaux Cave Paintings* (London: Faber and Faber, 1949), p. 12.

p. 102  Bataille, p. 129.

p. 103  "Ancient Aboriginal Art Discovered," BBCiNews, July 1, 2003, article reprinted at www.stonepages.com/news.

p. 106  Donald C. Johansen and Maitland A. Edey, *Lucy: The Beginnings of Humankind* (New York: Warner Books, 1981), p. 22.

p. 106  Johansen and Edey, p. 24.

p. 106  Johansen and Edey, p. 271.

p. 107  Tim Friend, "Skull Alters Notions of Human Origins," *USA Today,* July 11, 2002, p. 1A.

p. 107  Tim Friend, "Fossil Discovery Shakes Human Family Tree," *USA Today,* July 11, 2002, p. 5D.

p. 107  Guy Gugliotta, "Earliest Human Ancestor?" *The Washington Post,* July 11, 2002, pp. A1, A8.

p. 109  David Kennedy, *The Twin Towns of Zeugma on the Euphrates: Rescue Work and Historical Studies* (Portsmouth, RI: *Journal of Roman Archaeology,* 1998), p. 7.

p. 110  Interview with Gaetano Palumbo, "Last Ditch Archeology," PBS website (www.pbs.org/wgbh/nova/zeugma/salvage.html).

p. 111  Jim Campi, "Chancellorsville Project Opponents Plan Rally, March on December 14," *The Civil War News,* December 2002, p. 1.

p. 111  Kristen Stevens, "Archeology: Looking for Hidden Battlefields," *Hallowed Ground,* Summer 2002, p. 14.

p. 114  Albert A. Nofi, *The Gettysburg Campaign* (New York: Gallery Books, 1986), p. 187.

# For Further Information

## How to Become a Historian

The term "historian" has been used throughout this book, but there are actually many different kinds of professionals who interpret historical material. Usually **historians** work with written documents of the past; **archaeologists** dig up the materials from the past; **anthropologists** study human cultures and societies (**paleoanthropologists** work exclusively with early human cultures); **art historians** study the pictorial record of the past; and **museum curators** preserve and display the artifacts of the past. Although these are all fairly distinct fields, most historical research is shared among specialists. In addition, historical research often requires a great deal of scientific expertise, both for finding information and for the analysis of it—from people who provide radar to locate items underwater, to those who do the carbon dating or spectroanalysis of artifacts, to those whose specialty is stabilizing artifacts so that they can be exposed to the air. In order to become one of these specialists, you have to go to college and most likely to graduate school to get the skills you need to be part of the teams that investigate the past.

However, you can start now developing the kind of mind that will allow you to do that work later on. Start with the history that you are part of already—your own! Record stories from your family and even perhaps work on a family tree as a genealogist. Learn how to examine and handle artifacts by studying any heirlooms available in your own family. Learn how to evaluate historical documents by observing news coverage—pick a major news story to follow and see how coverage of it changes as time goes on. Watch how different people interpret the same information. This will prepare you to recognize bias and slant when you are working with historical documents.

Approach your local historical society or museum and ask if you can volunteer. This will expose you to other artifacts and documents and may even let you get your hands on the real materials of history. Organize or join an oral history project collecting the memories of old people in your community and become a real historian preserving this part of the past.

Finally, and most importantly, read about the things that interest you, either in books or on the Internet. The books below give more information about history and archaeology, and some websites could keep you exploring for years.

# Books

Burrell, Roy. *Oxford First Ancient History.* Oxford: Oxford University Press, 2000.

Devereux, Paul. *Archaeology: The Study of Our Past.* Milwaukee: Gareth Stevens, 2002.

*Dorling Kindersley Children's Atlas.* New York: DK Publishing, 2000.

Duke, Kate. *Archaeologists Dig for Clues.* New York: HarperCollins Children's Books, 1997.

McIntosh, Jane R. *Eyewitness: Archeology.* New York: DK Publishing, 2000.

Moloney, Norah. *The Young Oxford Book of Archaeology.* Oxford: Oxford University Press, 2000.

Panchyk, Richard. *Archaeology for Kids: Uncovering the Mysteries of Our Past.* Chicago: Chicago Review Press, 2001.

Steele, Phillip. *A City Through Time.* New York: DK Publishing, 2004.

Walker, Sally M. *Secrets of A Civil War Submarine: Solving the Mysteries of the H. L. Hunley.* Minneapolis: Carolrhoda Books, 2005.

Wheatley, Abigail, and Struan Reid. *The Usborne Introduction to Archaeology: Internet-Linked.* London: Usborne Books, 2005.

# Websites

*Archaeological News*
http://www.archaeologica.org/NewsPage.htm
Links to recent news articles about archaeology

*Archaeology*
http://www.archaeology.org
The official website of *Archaeology* magazine, a publication of the Archeological Institute of America

*Archaeo News*
http://www.stonepages.com/news
News summaries about recent archaeological digs and discoveries around the world

*The British Museum*
http://www.thebritishmuseum.ac.uk
"Compass" on the home page gives you access to photographs and information on more than five thousand objects in the museum collection

*Dig: The Archaeological Magazine for Kids*
http://www.digonsite.com/links.html
The links page of this site, by Cobblestone Publishing, sends the user to about fifty interesting archaeological sites. Topics include You Be the Historian, Walk through Time, Virtual Field Trip to Vesuvius, and the Museum of Ancient Inventions.

*Library of Congress—American Memory*
http://www.memory.loc.gov
Access point to the seven million digitized documents, maps, cartoons, photographs, etc., that are part of the Historical Collections of the National Digital Library

*National Archives*
http://www.archives.gov
"Research Room" on this page sends you to ARC, where you can find more than fifty-seven thousand photographs and fifteen thousand documents

# Index

Page numbers in *italics* refer to illustrations.

## Photo Acknowledgments

The photos in this book are used with the permission of: The Granger Collection, New York, pp. 7, 92 (bottom); National Archives, p. 11; Library of Congress, pp. 15 (left: LC-USZ62-11193, right: National American Woman Suffrage Association Collection), 16 (LC-DIG-cwpb-01095); © Archivo Iconografico, S.A./CORBIS, p. 17; © Adam Woolfitt/CORBIS, pp. 20, 68; Le Sault de Sainte Marie Historical Site, p. 22; © Bettmann/CORBIS, pp. 23, 65, 66, 81, 88, 105; Courtesy of the Smithsonian Institution, NMAH/Transportation, p. 29; Lake Champlain Maritime Museum, p. 30 (both); © Chris McLaughlin/CORBIS, p. 32; © North Wind Picture Archives, p. 34; Colonial Williamsburg Foundation, pp. 35, 36, 37; © Keren Su/CORBIS, p. 39;  American Museum of Natural History Library, Image #326597, p. 43; © Dave G. Houser/CORBIS, 45; © Sergio Dorantes/CORBIS, p. 46 (top); © Keith Dannemiller/CORBIS, p. 46 (bottom); © Daniel Aguilar/Reuters/CORBIS, p. 47; Scala/Art Resource, NY, p. 48; © Kevin Fleming/CORBIS, p. 51; © Richard A. Cooke/CORBIS, p. 52; © Ted Spiegel/CORBIS, p. 56; © Wolfgang Kaehler/CORBIS, p. 59 (top); © Tim Thompson/CORBIS, p. 59 (bottom); Bibliotheque Nationale, Paris, France/Bridgeman Art Library, p. 62; Bildarchiv Steffens/Bridgeman Art Library, p. 70; © Franz-Marc Frei/CORBIS, p. 71; INDEX/Bridgeman Art Library, pp. 74, 75; Bridgeman Art Library/Alinari, p. 76; © Mimmo Jodice/CORBIS, p. 77; © Jonathan Blair/CORBIS, p. 78; © Hulton-Deutsch Collection/CORBIS, p. 82; Ancient Art and Architecture Collection LTD/Bridgeman Art Library, p. 85; British Museum, London, UK/Bridgeman Art Library, p. 86; Museum of the City of New York/Bridgeman Art Library, p. 92 (top); © Chris Lisle/CORBIS, p. 96; © Sandro Vannini/CORBIS, p. 97; Bridgeman Art Library, p. 102; © Patrick Robert/CORBIS, p. 106; AP/Wide World Photos, pp. 110, 113; © STAN HONDA/AFP/Getty Images, p. 112.


Cover: Art Resource, NY (both).